σουλ

το

σουλ

(Soul to Soul)

By: Che' Clark

All Gold Publishing Co.
Dayton, Ohio

Copyright © 2016, by All Gold Publishing Co.

ISBN 0-9701519-0-X

Published by All Gold Publishing Co.

P.O. Box 13504

Dayton, OH 45413

http://www.allgoldpublishing.com

Printed in the United States of America.

Cover Design: Warren C. Amos

Text Design: Warren C. Amos

Copy Editors: Tammy Cvetnic and Margaret Rice

This book is dedicated *to a*
Wonderful Man.
"Mr. Charles Talley"

Acknowledgments and Thanks

There were many people who made this book possible, and I would like to thank you all. Special thanks go out to Margaret Rice for her faith and belief in me, to her friends, Dorothy Beatty and Vicki Gulley for their voluntary assistance. To Tammi Cvetnic for her hard work and dedication in editing and proofreading. And Special thanks also go out to Larry O'Donnell for his review of and comments. And lastly I praise and thank the Lord for providing me with the great **D**iscipline, **O**rganization, and **E**ducation that made this project possible.

*Where appropriate, places, dates and character names
have been changed to protect the innocent.*

Prologue

Life starts out so perfect and normal. The grass is green and pretty, the home that you live in is warm and safe, and you never go hungry or naked. You feel like you have it all. The people that seem to be less fortunate look in amazement because your life is a dream to them. But if they knew what went on inside, they would not trade places with you for the world.

That's how it was for this family who seemed to have it all. They always had five or more living generations that were fairly wealthy compared to others in their neighborhood. All of them were very attractive people who could not help but to be the center of attention. People from the outside thought the members of this family did not have a worry in the world. Everything financially and materially was handed down to them from generation to generation. As time went on, and more new generations were created, they too thought that everything was going to be handed to them. But then it happened, the first male child to lead a generation was born into this family. The family feared Young Gold in a godly way because he was different. They knew from the time he left the hospital he was special because he had a golden glow to him. Up until he reached manhood he thought he had been born into high royalty just like everyone else in the family. But when Young Gold saw why everyone loved his family, he asked God if his life would ever be normal.

The family that Young Gold was born into had been without a model male figure for many generations. That's why the beautiful women in his family attracted a lot of attention. Men from outside of the family saw them as easy prey. They controlled the women in Gold's family with drugs, money, and all of the material things that looked good from the outside. It was not until Young Gold was born that these women's hearts were filled with the love they had never received from their great-grandfathers, grandfathers and their fathers. Young Gold watched and studied the men who brought enormous pain and abuse to the women around him. With the help of God and his guardian angel he felt that he had to do something to show the women in his family they had a real man in their lives. And most importantly, he wanted to make sure that the lifestyle of the past generations was not passed down to his own generation and the one to follow.

Chapter 1

On Friday, September 13, 1974, at 3:03 p.m. Roland C. Gold made history. Going back as far as anyone could remember, the first born child of a generation had always been female. He became the first child to lead a generation being a male child on his mother's side of the family. With him breaking this family tradition, he became very special to the women in his family. And the fact that there were no responsible men in the family to perform the masculine duties made him even more special to them. The women in Young Gold's family now had their own man who they could mold to become the backbone of their family. They held very high expectations for him. Sesame Street's Big Bird didn't stack up to the guitar, drum, and piano lessons he received between the ages of three and five. The women were preparing him for the real world, and what it would take for him to become a successful and responsible man. Learning and education was at the top of their list. His grandma always insisted, "An education is the one thing a person cannot take away from you. Once you plant it in your head, it's yours." It was important to them that Young Gold be instilled with the proper discipline necessary for learning.

The next important thing to these women was family, and theirs was missing a valuable part, the men. Now that they had their own, nothing would ever stand in the way of infusing him with responsibility, commitment, and discipline in order to make him a leader. The women of Gold's family hoped, prayed, and held faith that they would remain strong long enough for Young Gold to reach the stage where he would be labeled chief of their clan. Once he obtained such status, there would be no dependency on men from outside the family or from the irresponsible men who were already connected to the family.

Gold's highly accelerated growing and learning years were spent with his great-great grandma, Rosey Allen; his great-grandma, Anita K. Brent; his grandma, April K. Cole; his mother, Sparkle H. Hoover; and his three aunts, Rachel, Mica, and China Hoover. On the other side, he spent very little to no bonding time with the men in his family. His great-great-grandfather Kilmery C. Brent was born on a plantation in a case where the slave owner got one of his slaves' pregnant. With his father being already married, and a respected white slave owner of Irish descent, the truth never came out about him being Kilmery's father. Kilmery C. Brent carried his father's last name only because at that time it was a law that most slaves carried the last name of their owner. Even though his father did not legally claim him, Kilmery C. Brent was raised with high stature because he easily passed as a white child. He was welcomed in his owner's home, and received many special privileges that other plantation children were denied. His father was very wealthy, and owned many plantations in the south. Kilmery C. Brent probably could have lived a long prosperous life, but he and Rosey, Young Gold's great-great grandmother was force to marry early in their teenage years after giving birth to Anita.

It was told that Kilmery C. Brent had died shortly after Anita reached aged two, and just a month before Rosey gave birth to a son who she named Kilmery C. Brent Jr. The only first hand knowledge that Young Gold had about his great-great grandfather had been he say she say. And this information was nothing more than characteristics about his appearance. At fifteen all Rosey knew was what she was told, and that was that her husband Kilmery C. Brent was dead.

Gold's great-great grandma Rosey, Anita, Kilmery Jr., her siblings, and her parents continued to move north fighting slavery when she was introduce to her second husband Henry James. Rosey and Henry James married in Cincinnati, Ohio shortly after he was released from the army. He had not long been back in the United States from France because of his heroic participation in the First World War. They moved to Dayton, where they gave birth to nine children of their own, seven surviving while two were stillborn. Since Anita and Kilmery Jr. had no remembrance of their father, Henry James excepted them as his despite their complexion difference from their siblings. One would not know that Anita and Kilmery Jr. had a different father from the others because Henry treated them just as equal as his own. Besides, Henry was the only father that they had ever known.

When the family referred to Gold's great-great grandfather they were giving mention to Henry. Gold heard stories of how great of a man he was, but he had also passed a way before Gold was born. Gold's great-grandfather, Flip Cole, died when Gold was twelve. Prior to the day Young Gold and his Grandma April went to identify Flip's body lying dead on his living room floor, Young Gold had seen his great-grandfather only twice. His grandfather, L.C Hoover, was a dedicated working man who had started a family with another woman. It was her influence that drove him to come into Young Gold's life shortly after Flip died. But not being there from day one made a huge difference in their relationship. They never grew as close as a grandfather and a first born grandchild should have. Gold's father, Brad J. Gold, simply did not make time for him. Gold didn't rank among his father's list of priorities. And of his three uncles, Lenny, Eric, and Ward Hoover, Gold spent the most time with Lenny, the one with fewest male role model qualities. Even though he was eighteen years older than Gold, he was just as dependent on the women in the family as Gold was.

Lenny shacked house to house living with his grandmother, mother, and two of his three sisters. This made Gold treat him like a cousin instead of an uncle. Gold's Uncle Eric was sentenced to prison for twenty-five years for murder when Young Gold was seven. Gold visited Eric often for the first five years of his sentence, but as Young Gold got older, prison was a place he tried to avoid altogether. His Uncle Ward was the only child from his grandfather's second marriage, but that had nothing to do with the lack of time that he and Young Gold spent together. Ward was putting his energy into a successful football career at a big time university, and if he could have overcame a troublesome knee injury, the professional level would have been in reach.

There was so little male leadership and manhood in Young Gold's family that the women looked forward to Young Gold's future contributions. Yet, until he reached the stage where he could provide for them and lead them, they had to deal with the unbalanced support of the men that were involved. Handling tremendous household and family responsibilities alone was a struggle. Most of the fight was fought at close range trying to keep the men connected to the family. With rapid blows thrown, the men threw in the towel before the final bell of the last round, forcing the women to find male companionship outside of the ring, and in most bouts, looking for love in all the wrong places.

Chapter 2

After Young Gold's parents split up in 1977 Sparkle kept her mind strong, and held her ground to ensure Young Gold a bright future. They moved in with Gold's Grandma April for a few months until they found a place of their own. At three, Gold was too young to understand what was going on, but he knew he was spending less time with his father and more time with the women in his family. His mother and father messed around a little after their split up, but it wasn't strong enough to pull them back together. They were only trying to please Gold, and make the separation easier for him.

Gold spent some weekends at his father's house, but the time they shared together was limited. Brad J. Gold was too busy running the streets and chasing women to spend time with his son. He placed the responsibility on his mother, Honey Gold, and his sister, Lisa. They were the ones who made sure Young Gold was bathed, clothed, and fed on his weekend visits. Brad only participated in Gold's life on Christmas and Thanksgiving. And even then, all Brad did was deliver and assemble a new bike or some toy. He never spent any father - son quality time with Young Gold. There were no games played, no balls thrown, and no male guidance provided during their visits. But Sparkle didn't worry. She believed that even without the guidance of his father Young Gold would grow into a strong, independent, responsible man who would take care of her and his family.

Sparkle was very attractive, intelligent, and hard working. She did it all: modeling, sewing, bartending, home interior decorating, and single parenting. The pace of her life was usually too fast to worry about a man. Gold's father was the first man she gave her heart and love to. The one she gave her virginity to. She was hurt that the relationship didn't work, but most of her pain came from Brad not being a responsible father to his child. Sparkle knew how it felt to grow up without a father, so she followed in her mother's footsteps. She moved on to fulfill her dreams, and only involved herself with men who were interested in Gold as well as in her.

Chapter 3

The first man Sparkle brought into Young Gold's life besides his father was a man named Silver. She got involved with him about three years after she and Young Gold's father spilt up. In the beginning, their relationship was more business than pleasure. He was remodeling beautiful elegant tri-level homes, and she was doing high-class interior decorating work. Their professions were complimentary, like paint and unfinished drywall. Even though Silver was already involved with a woman, he could not help but to saw a little off of the chalk line. Gold was six when he met Silver. Gold viewed him as a positive male role model. The strong, independent type of man he wanted to be when he was older. A man with fast cars, a young girlfriend studying to become a nurse, a couple of mature lady-friends on the side, a big self-remodeled home, with a pool room, basketball court, and weight room. Silver had all of the material things that made a man cool.

Silver played more of an uncle role in Young Gold's life rather than that of a stepfather. He spent valuable time with Gold, treating him like a true friend at a young age. The twenty-four year old age difference between them made no difference in their relationship. He taught Gold all about sports, cars, and construction. He was one of the first men to inspire Young Gold to journey and to take chances in life. He always told Gold, "Don't be afraid of new experiences, just stay focused. Some places and goals seem far away, but if you stay focused, you can get or do anything you want." Some weekends Silver would take Young Gold and his own son Gene to some of Dayton's larger neighboring cities like Cincinnati and Indianapolis. The boys fell in love with the big buildings, bright lights, and pretty women walking though the down-town streets. The trips to Cincinnati's Enon Park were like a stroll around the corner. It was only forty minutes from Dayton. And with Silver driving, it seemed to be twenty minutes away. Gold and Gene begged to go there every weekend.

Gold and Gene clicked from the first day they met. They always competed in basketball and pool on their visits at Silver's house. Gene was twelve and Gold was seven, so Gene usually had the edge. Silver and Gene's mother were not always on good terms, so the boys' time together was limited. Gene's mother kept Gene distant from his father because she thought Silver had changed drastically after his girlfriend Tia died.

In 1981, Silver lost Tia during an argument. She went for a gun. Silver attempted to disarm her, but during the scuffle there was a loud bang. Tia dropped to the floor in the hallway. As soon as Silver saw the blood from her mid-section, he knew she was dead. He was blamed for her death from all directions. Her family members and friends held him responsible. His family and friends held him responsible, all because of his involvement with drugs. The law strongly investigated Tia's death as a homicide, but there was not enough evidence to make a case. Silver became stressed to the point where he also started to blame himself. Tia was surely the most important person in Silver's life, and the most important woman ever, next to his mother, who had died during his early teenage years.

With Tia gone, Silver lost all control of his life. He felt that he didn't have anyone left in his world. He hated his father for not having shared his mother's financial assets with him and his brother. Through the tragedy of losing Tia, Silver had no loved ones to support him or help him ease the pain and hurt that was bottled up inside. Instead of going on with his life and continuing to chase his dreams, he released his pain in drugs and violence. It was near that time that Young Gold's and Silver's relationship rolled off the roof like rain into the gutter.

Sparkle was doing interior decorating work at a friend's nightclub in Columbus around the time Tia died. If anyone knew how Silver cared for Tia, Sparkle did. She knew Silver needed a shoulder on which to mourn, and she let him bow his head onto hers. She put a lot of energy into Silver because she did not want to see a strong polished man fade. But he abused the trust and support Sparkle gave him, instead of taking advantage of it. He let the drugs get the best of him. At first, Sparkle did not notice that Silver's drug habit was a problem because he could afford it. When his money started to decline, so did his life. He stayed behind the steel curtain as long as he could, but the drugs ate through him like acid. He had lost all the things that were once important to him: Tia, his drive, his son, and finally Young Gold and Sparkle. The strong man who was a creative father to Gene and an uncle figure to Young Gold became weak. He let the evil inside of him take over to survive his pain.

Sparkle stood by Silver's side a little longer, hoping he would snap back, but it only pulled her down with him. As time passed in their relationship, she went from smoking a little marijuana to experimenting with cocaine. For his own selfishness, Silver talked her into getting some coke from her friends in Columbus. He said to her, "Get them to give you some cane and I can put some extra money in your pocket." With her being vulnerable at the time, she went along with Silver's plan. He was the only one who knew where she stashed the cocaine when she got it. Silver plotted the whole thing out. He came to pick her up one night around 9:30 to go out for a drink. About five minutes after they pulled down the street, Silver's buddy went to the stash spot and got the drugs. When Sparkle and Silver came back to the apartment, Sliver asked her to give him a line before he went home. She went to her hiding spot to get the package, and it was gone. They looked all over the house for about three hours and then Silver said, "Someone must have got it because the damn bag is not in here." Sparkle knew she wasn't crazy, and she knew that Silver was the only person who knew where the coke was.

Later that week Sparkle's friends from Columbus came to town to collect their money. She told them what had happened, but they did not believe her. They figured she had something to do with it, so they held her and Young Gold at gunpoint and threatened to kill them if Silver was not found. Sparkle took the men to Silver's house, but he did not have the drugs or the money. After receiving several gunshot wounds, broken ribs, and head injuries that required a metal plate to be placed in his forehead, Silver confessed to stealing the drugs. The men were going to kill him, but Sparkle spared his life. The brutal beating was not only about the drugs. It had more to do with the fact that Silver had crossed a good woman and put her child's life in danger. They wanted to kill Silver for being a coward and leaving Sparkle and Young Gold to pay with their lives for his actions.

A year later Silver's dirt continued to catch up with him. He was dating a white woman far out in the country. Her husband and three of his friends followed Silver from a gas station in town one night. When Silver turned onto the country road that led to the woman's house, the men in the black pick-up truck smashed into him from behind. Silver had no idea that it was the white woman's husband, so he sped up, racing to her house for safety. Once he got inside the men began to beat on the door. The woman then told Silver who it was, so he armed himself with a butcher knife. As the woman's husband kicked through the door, Silver stabbed him in the abdomen. The other three men ran back to the truck and fled. The woman dialed 911. Then Silver tried to take off, but his car was not mobile because the white men had smashed it with their pick-up truck. He took off on foot, but he was more than twenty miles from the city and the police quickly tracked him down. Silver insisted that it was a case of self-defense, but he didn't stand a chance because of the incident with Tia a year before. The Judge gave him something of a break, because he was only sentenced to three years in prison. Sparkle lost all respect for Silver, but at the same time she felt sorrow because he wasted the good life he once had.

Chapter 4

Sparkle was slowly cutting her involvement with drugs, but her environment was holding her back. She and Gold were living in a perfect fit two-bedroom apartment off N. Main Street. An Oldsmobile used-car dealership separated their apartment from the local burger joint where the neighborhood prostitutes hung out. She had been friends with most of the drug dealers who supplied the city's pimps with drugs for their prostitutes. The girls would hear Sparkle's name mentioned during conversations between their pimps and different dealers. All the pimps wanted to know who she was because of the classy, sophisticated manner in which she carried herself. She was the type of woman that most pimps dreamed about. It was known in the streets that she was an authoritative, self-controlled woman who was the niece of one of the biggest pimps in Dayton during the seventies. Still, this did not stop them from trying to recruit Sparkle. Despite efforts using other prostitutes and their own pimp charm, they all fell short, only gaining a small bit of her friendship and acquaintance.

From the research the prostitutes did trying to get Sparkle involved in their line of work, they found out she had connections with the big name cocaine dealers. Instead of taking trick money to their pimps at the end of the night, they began to take it to Sparkle for coke. This way they could control their own habit instead of having dope rationed out to them by their pimps. The prostitutes felt comfortable dealing with a woman because the chance of their pimps finding out about their side drug use was less risky. With Silver out of the picture, Sparkle would now call a guy name B.J when the girls came for a fix. He was a married family man who worked for General Motors on second shift and sold cocaine on the side. It was hard for him to leave his house after certain hours because his wife was suspicious. To keep her out of his secret life, he would leave small amounts of his product with Sparkle, or send someone else to her house when she called for the girls. Young Gold did not know anything about B.J and his mother's relationship with drugs. At seven, Gold did not even know that drugs were called drugs. He thought B.J was trying to be his mother's new boyfriend since Silver was gone. Every Thursday on his lunch break, B.J would take Gold downtown to play video games in some hotel where he cashed his check. And every Friday before he went to work, he brought Sparkle money to buy pizza.

One Friday night while waiting for the pizza man, Young Gold heard a car door close and went to the kitchen window to see if it was the pizza man. The police had been watching the prostitutes from the fenced in Oldsmobile used-car dealership parking lot for about three months. They saw the prostitutes regularly coming and going to Sparkle's apartment and suspected drug activity was going on. That Friday, the police set up a sting operation. They watched for dealers bringing drugs in, and prostitutes taking them out. Just after Sparkle had ordered pizza, a woman came looking for twenty-five dollars worth of coke. Friday nights was Sparkle's bonding time with Young Gold, and she didn't get involved in transactions on those nights unless Gold was already gone to his grandma's or his great-grandma's for the weekend.

When Gold looked out the window he yelled, "Mom, there are a lot of white men with guns outside, and they got that woman who just left!" Five minutes later the police were beating down the security door to get to the door that led to Sparkle's apartment. They kicked the door and screamed, "Police, open the door!" Sparkle had nothing to hide, so she opened the door. The cop with the search warrant was polite. He tried to explain in a mannerly way what was going on, and what they were looking for while the other twenty cops ransacked the apartment yelling, "Bitch, where's the drugs and the money?" They had found less than a half gram of cocaine on the woman they had stopped outside and were looking for the rest of the drugs and the marked bills the woman claimed to have given Sparkle. Young Gold was a nervous wreck. He thought the men were going to kill him and his mother. They had on everyday clothes, so he didn't understand they were the police. Gold thought they were white mobsters like the black men who held him and his mother at gunpoint when Silver stole the drugs. The police officer in charge took Young Gold to his bedroom to settle him down. The officer said quietly, "Everything's going to be all right. No one is going to get hurt." Then asked, "Do you know where your mother keeps the white powder at?" Gold sobbed "no" with tears dripping off his face. The only items the police found in the raid were an unloaded 22-caliber pistol, a small piece of a Marijuana joint, half of a Valium pill and the twelve dollars for the pizza man. Nothing listed on the search warrant was found. The police concluded that the woman who came out of the apartment already had the drugs on her when she entered Sparkle's place, and lied to them because she didn't want to go down by herself.

The police caused hundreds of dollars worth of unnecessary damage to the apartment, and placed a scar on Young Gold that would last a lifetime. He no longer thought of the police as someone you called for protection or help. They were now an organization he feared. And the nightmares he continued to have years after the police raid did not help ease his mind about the police. This was the last straw for Sparkle. She could not continue living the dangerous street life, putting Gold's promising life at stake. She had to change for the sake of her child.

With Sparkle's life being so far left of center, she knew it was going to takes progressive steering to get back to the middle of the road from which she had started. She did not expect things to change overnight. But to start over again her once successful life, she went on the grind for about six months, working a dead end job preparing food for nursing home patents. B.J claimed he felt bad about the police raiding her apartment that Friday night. To show his sympathy, he started spending more time with her and Gold than with his own family. But this made Sparkle uncomfortable because he was still married. She was trying to move forward with her life. The little odd end job was a start to her efforts to change her lifestyle. She found a house near the business district of Dayton and centered in a quiet Jewish neighborhood just around the corner from her mother's dream house. This move felt like a great thing to Sparkle because she desperately desired a new environment. Now she only had to untie the tangles in her relationship with B.J. It was time for him to be with her or his wife, not both.

It was not a pressured situation. Sparkle gave B.J as much space, and time as he needed to get his end compatible with hers. She knew he had to take his four children -- Roxy, who was sixteen; Brian, fourteen; Dave, twelve; and Ray, four -- into consideration before making divorce decisions. So she continued making necessary changes in her life which would not be influenced either way by B.J's decision.

Since Sparkle was already working, her next step was to save some money for the house she had found. The nursing home was giving her more hours, and a preacher associated with the nursing home found odd jobs around the church for her. He saw how hard she was trying to turn her life around and always had work for her. He also knew about her situation with B.J. "Just have faith that everything will turn out alright with him. But no matter what happens between you and your male friend, Gold is the only man you need to be concerned about," he preached all the time. He was being the positive male or father figure Sparkle needed in her life during her rehabilitation.

About three weeks went by, and there was no sign of B.J. Gold asked one day, "When is B.J coming over?" His mother responded with an unexpected look on her face, "I don't know, I guess he had a change of heart." Being only seven, Gold did not know exactly what that meant, but he had some idea. Shortly after Gold asked that question, his mother's mind started racing with serious thoughts, thinking B.J could be hurt, in jail, or maybe working things out with his wife. But to Sparkle, none of those were legitimate reasons for him not contacting her.

Earlier that day one of Sparkle's male friends called to see if she and Gold wanted to go check out a movie at the drive-in. There was a special -- three movies on both screens. She was still puzzled after Gold's question about B.J, and wondered where he was, so she told her friend she'd let him know later. When something troubled her, she would constantly clean up around the house, do some rearranging, or remodeling. That day, after everything was spic'n'span, B.J was still on her mind. She needed something to get him off her mind, so she called her friend back and told him, "A movie would be perfect for the way I'm feeling right now." He replied, "Great, I'll see you around eight."

That night, after the movie, Sparkle's friend dropped her and Gold off in the back of their apartment building. They had to walk around to the front in order to enter. Young Gold was half-asleep stumbling along, and Sparkle was dragging him in a hurry because it was pitch dark on the side of the building. As they climbed the four small cement steps attempting to unlock the security door, B.J appeared in the dark from behind. He grabbed Sparkle by the arm spinning her around to face him, then shouted, "Bitch, where have you been, and who dropped you off?" Before she could get the first syllable of the first word out of her mouth, he began slapping her several times in the head as she ducked her face. She cried in shock, unlocking the door to send Gold upstairs with the key to the apartment to prevent him from witnessing any more of the attack. Young Gold had never seen a man hit his mother or any other woman before. But he knew it was not a normal interaction between men and women. The next morning the whole fight was like an image of a bad dream. Gold barely remembered it as something that had actually occurred because he had been only half-awake. Also, B.J was in his mother's bed that morning, so he convinced himself it was all a bad dream. But it was a dream he would never quite forget.

B.J apologized to Sparkle, telling her his wife had been stressing him out, and he did not mean to take it out on her. The stress from his wife may have had a little to do with his actions, but it was mostly jealously. He couldn't accept that Sparkle went to a movie with another man. Now he understood somewhat of how she felt with him being married. The only way Sparkle would accept his apology and continue their relationship was with proof of divorce papers. B.J knew he had to comply with her wishes, or his relationship with her would end.

Leaving his wife really was not a problem because their marriage had been going downhill for the last two years. His main problem was making the transition easy for his children. The three oldest children knew about their father's relationship with Sparkle, and the marital problems between their parents, but were not happy with the situation. His youngest son, Ray, was the one having trouble understanding what was going on. To give him some understanding of the situation, B.J started bringing Ray around Gold and Sparkle, hoping he would get used to them and understand that they were going to be a part of his life. But with Ray being mama's and daddy's baby boy, he did not accept his father spending time with another woman and her son. When B.J brought Ray around Sparkle, Ray used foul language, and did not following directions, and was very disobedient. Sparkle did not accept this sort of behavior from Gold, and she refused to accept it from any other child, so she did not take much liking to Ray. But his misbehavior was not all his fault. He couldn't help it that his mother taught him to misbehave when or if his father took him around other women. One of her favorites was to tell Ray to call the women the 'B' word when he was in their presence. Basically he acted like the average four year-old child whose parents were on the verge of an ugly divorce.

B.J's wife knew he was leaving her for another woman because the children had told her about Sparkle. It wasn't a secret anymore, the divorce was well in motion, and B.J was now trying to make the best accommodations for his children to start a new life with him, Sparkle, and Young Gold. His wife could accept his leaving her, but there was no forgiveness for his ruining her beautiful family, only wishes for him to catch hell for the rest of his life. She refused to participate in any more clown shows in B.J's circus and took Ray and went to stay with her sister until the divorce was final. The three oldest children, Roxy, Brian, and Dave stayed with their father while the house and all the furnishings were being sold. Things did not turn out too badly for B.J, he thought. His wife left him with three of their four children, and now he figured it was time for him and Sparkle to join the children and start a new family. But before things came together, the devil caught up with him. It was as if his wife had a personal conversation with the devil and asked him to grant her a special wish.

One Friday night after work, B.J went to Sparkle's house to rest a while before heading home. Just before he dozed off, he received a heated phone call. It was Sparkle's sister Rachel on the line. "Let me speak to B.J," she demanded. "What do you want with him?" Sparkle responded. "I got these two white men down here, and B.J told me that him and his brother M.D was looking for a easy lick," she claimed. Before handing B.J the telephone, Sparkle thought about telling Rachel he was gone, or in the shower, anything to avoid her from talking to him. Sparkle knew her sister was not the brightest of stars and that when someone went along with one of her crazy plans, they usually ended up severely hurt, dead, in jail, or wanted. Young Gold sat back on the couch watching television as if he was not paying any attention to B.J's telephone conversation. He heard B.J ask, "Do they have any guns?" And from that moment on, Gold did not let one word pass by his maturing ears. He smelled action in the air, and refused to let the aroma pass his nose. After B.J hung up with Rachel he called his brother, M.D, "Are you ready?" he asked, emotionally aroused. "Ready for what?" M.D replied. "Sparkle's sister, Rachel got two rich white men at her house with a bank roll of money, gold chains, and diamond rings." He also added that the men did not have any guns. With M.D living a hard-knocks life, this was right up his alley. He had robbed people, beat people, killed people, been shot multiple times, been to prison, and faced everything under the sun a mad man could face, so robbing two unarmed white men sounded like easy pickings. But since he was a real gangster, he didn't underestimate the opposition. He loaded his 12-gauge sawed-off shotgun and his 45-magnum as he would have for any criminal act, and waited for B.J to pick him up.

In the meantime, B.J was listening to Sparkle tell him how stupid the whole robbery idea was. "You don't know the danger you're facing getting involved with Rachel," she told him. Sparkle knew the situations her sister would put people in. There were many occasions when Sparkle had fell victim to her sister's stupidity. Sparkle was trying to explain to B.J that most of Rachel's actions and decisions were made without forethought. She had lived on the edge all her life. With her being fearless she took action first and worried about the consequences when they caught up with her. Nothing Sparkle said changed B.J's mind. He marched out of the apartment courageously as if he was going to win a war.

B.J and M.D pulled up in front of Rachel's house. The two white men sat in their car across the street, in front of Rachel's grandmother's house waiting for her. Rachel and B.J had already discussed the plan over the telephone. B.J pretended to bring pampers to Sparkle's and Rachel's grandmother's house for one of the kids. The bag did have a few pampers in it, but the weight came from his nickel-plated 38-caliber pistol. M.D bent down in the front seat with his guns loaded, waiting for B.J to come out of the house and give him the signal.

When B.J came out of the house, he gave a low muffled whistle as he approached the passenger side of the men's car. In no time M.D had his sawed-off shotgun in the face of the driver. They demanded they hand over their money and jewelry. Shortly after the two men began handing B.J and M.D their possessions, they started shooting. B.J was hit in his side. It was a natural instinct for M.D to shoot to kill when he heard the gun shots, and the fact that his brother was hit made it certain both men must die, so he unloaded on them as he back-paddled for cover. Both of the men were hit, but only one of them was dead. There was no time to finish off the passenger because B.J was bleeding badly, and the police were in route. It was just like Sparkle had explained to B.J. Rachel's homework was insufficient, and the men had been pre-pared for any danger in their path. They were not ordinary rich white men. They were bodyguards for a most lethal and notorious gangster, who operated out of Dayton.

Rachel, B.J, and M.D were in an outright panic because the robbery hadn't gone as planned, but that was just the beginning of their problems. All the way to the hospital they fussed and cussed: "I thought you said they didn't have any guns." "If you wouldn't have brought him it would have worked." "Just drop me off," the three argued. When they got B.J to the hospital, the nurses and doctors asked Rachel how he got shot. She told them, "I don't know. I just heard gun shots outside my grandmother's house, and when I went outside, my sister's boyfriend asked me to drive him to the hospital." They knew she was lying and called the police and left matters in their hands. M.D knew the hospital would call the police; that's why he wanted to get dropped off before they got there. All he could do was hide out and hope his brother would be fine.

Shortly after the doctors removed the bullet from B.J's side, he and Rachel faced their next problem – answering pesky police and detectives questions. B.J was still unconscious, but when he came to, he would find he had to deal with the police by himself. When Rachel saw them entering B.J's room; she quickly disappeared like she was an assistant in a magician's magic trick. She fled from the hospital heading to Sparkle's house to inform her of the situation, and to tell her the bad news. But first she picked up her boyfriend, Buzz, who had also been involved in plotting the robbery. They pulled up in the back of Sparkle's apartment so B.J's car would not be spotted. When Sparkle saw them without B.J she instantly knew something was wrong. "I told him to leave M.D at home, if he wouldn't have brought him everything would have went smoothly," Rachel argued frantically. Sparkle just asked one question, "Where is B.J?" Rachel got the word hospital out of her mouth and Sparkle yelled, "Every time someone deals with you, something bad happens! Get out!" Rachel and Buzz left looking for a place to hide out. They had most of the money and jewelry from the robbery in their possession, so they went downtown to stay in a motel.

Back at the hospital all hell was breaking loose for B.J. The passenger who was shot in the robbery had just arrived at the same hospital, which made the detectives' job very easy. After the man told his story and described the shooters involved, the detectives put two and two together and went to B.J's room for some answers. It did not take long for them to convince B.J they had witnesses who said he was involved in an altercation that killed one man and wounded another. And when they told him the wounded man was a couple of doors down, he knew the heat was on. He had to decide if he was going to take the heat by himself, or tell the detectives what they wanted to know about the other players involved in the robbery. With the main witness in the same hospital as B.J, he felt the only chance he had to avoid prison was to put the robbery and the shooting on Rachel and Buzz. He did not want to go down for armed robbery, and he did not want his brother to go down for armed robbery and murder, so he told the detectives that Rachel had set the whole thing up, and her boyfriend had done the shooting.

The police felt there was some truth to his story, but the man shot on the passenger side of the car during the robbery claimed there were only two men present, and with B.J being shot they knew he had to be one of those men. There was no way to explain how or why he got shot if Rachel and Buzz did all of the dirty work. So, at last, the detectives left to find Rachel and her boyfriend, so they could get the story straight.

The detectives set-up stakeouts at Rachel's house and at her children's school bus stop. They figured if anyone knew where she was, her children did, but the police were mistaken because the kids had not seen her in over a week. She and her boyfriend had left the motel and went to hide out in B.J's and M.D's parents' basement. Their money was getting low and B.J's family did not want Rachel and Buzz to tell the police what had really happened. But being shacked up in the basement didn't last long. Buzz was the first to leave. "I haven't done anything wrong, they don't have nothing on me," he argued to Rachel. She replied, "You fool go ahead. I'm not going anywhere." Within two hours the police had Buzz in custody. He was caught just around the corner from Rachel's house.

Of course, he told all that had happened except the parts that he had participated in. The information he gave was accurate, but still not the truth. He told the detectives, "Rachel met the white man that got killed when we split up downtown early that day. The man told her he had a friend coming to town that night, and that he might be interested in some women. When they got to Rachel's house, B.J and his brother were waiting to rob them." This was the first time M.D's name came up in the investigation, so now the detectives had another person to find besides Rachel.

While the detectives had Buzz in the interrogation room, they sent two police units to M.D's last known address and to his parents' house. "You know you're facing armed robbery and murder charges," one of the detectives warned Buzz. He responded shaking nervous, "I didn't kill anybody." "We were told you did the shooting and Rachel set up the robbery," bluffed the detective. Buzz was trying to avoid telling the detectives anything they didn't already know, so he kept denying his involvement. Besides, he was use to the police's interrogation system. He had current warrants, and a lengthy criminal background.

Two and a half weeks passed before Rachel finally surfaced. One early morning Rachel arrived at her grandmother's house where the robbery took place. She suspected she was being followed because she saw a car pull up just as she entered the house. She quickly jumped in the shower, changed her clothes, and hid in the closet. About five minutes later there was a knock on the door. "Is Rachel Hoover here?" someone asked in a deep intimidating voice. Rachel's grandmother didn't want to be involved, but she also didn't want to see anything happen to her granddaughter, so she told them Rachel wasn't there. The detectives knew she was lying and asked, "Do you mind if we search the house for ourselves?" Rachel's grandmother cooperated because she did not want to get into any trouble. The detectives came in and searched the house, but they could not find Rachel. So they just drove to the end of the corner, out of sight, to wait for her to come out.

Rachel's grandmother was disturbed and upset by the whole ordeal and she put Rachel out of her house shortly after the detectives left. Rachel strolled down the street puzzling over a destination with her face covered with a newspaper as if she was reading. Her disguise was obvious, but she somehow managed to walk right past the detectives' car. As soon as she threw the paper down, thinking she was in the clear, the detectives turned the corner and jumped out on her. They took her to the station for questioning. With the testimony Rachel gave them, the investigation was nearing an end. Rachel was tired of running, so she told the detectives everything they wanted to know in return for her freedom. Her wish was easy for them to grant. With the information she had, they could build a case against B.J and M.D that would guarantee both of them fifteen or more years in prison.

Since B.J had no prior criminal record and a good job, the judge let him out on bail during the trial. Sparkle and Young Gold had already moved into their new house, and were well on their way to starting a life in a positive direction. For the first three weeks, the house was fairly empty. The furnishings she brought from their two-bedroom apartment across the street from the Oldsmobile used car lot did not nearly fill the space of this enormous three-bedroom house. She was not in a big rush to fully furnish the house, she was merely happy to be settled. She took one room at a time, but Gold's room was her first concern. He had to sleep in her room during those first three weeks because he didn't have a mattress and box spring for his bed. This gave her incentive to stay up at night and decorate other areas of the house since her resting quarters were being occupied by Gold. This was the first house she lived in since she was out on her own. The two apartments she had lived in before had both been decorated with some of her best interior decorating designs, but now she had more room to display her talent.

Sparkle did not spend a lot of time preparing for the move after the shooting incident. She feared that friends of the white men involved in the shooting might try to retaliate against B.J. When he came home he was bothered because he wanted to be a part of Sparkle's transition into her new life and her new environment. The move made him wonder if she would be there for him while he was in prison. There was no fooling himself: he knew eventually he would have to serve jail time, and the fact remained that he was still married. Now he had to figure out a way to keep Sparkle in his corner until the divorce was final, and until he got home from prison. But it all really depended on how many years he would have to serve.

B.J's days were numbered. Time was running out as his pre-trial hearing quickly approached. If he had listened to Sparkle in the beginning, he wouldn't have had to face the problems ahead of him. The preacher Sparkle worked for was proud of her accomplishments and continued to help out during the trying times. He saw to it that Young Gold's bedroom was fully furnished, and even tried to help B.J during his trial. "You might make a better impression on the judge if he knows that you and your family are members of the church, and that you're a man of God" Mr. Smith suggested. B.J knew if anyone could help him fight through the mess, the Lord could. Mr. Smith welcomed B.J, Sparkle, and B.J's mother as members of his church. Since B.J had a good job, no prior criminal record, and was a member of the church, his chances were much greater of getting a sentence less than the usual for armed robbery and attempted murder. But he still had a lot of unfinished business on top of the new mess he had created for himself.

One good thing did happen for B.J during this hardship. His wife was finally convinced that things were over between them. She signed the divorce papers, took the two youngest children, and moved to Texas. Roxy and Brian, the two oldest children, were well on their way to being adults. She figured it would be in their best interest to stay with their father for disciplinary reasons. This opened the door for B.J to make the move he had been planning before he got into his troublesome situation – him, his two teenagers, Sparkle, and Gold living together as one big happy family. He also figured this would better the chance of Sparkle waiting on him until he came home from prison.

Things worked out perfectly for B.J, but it was a little more than Sparkle, Young Gold, and his children had expected. B.J moved his living room furniture, Brian's and Roxy's bedroom suites, and some kitchen appliances that hadn't sold from his old house into Sparkle's home to fill the empty space left in many of the rooms. Roxy had her own room, which Brian and Gold thought was unfair, but she was the oldest and the only girl. Young Gold was really upset. Before they invaded he had a bedroom to himself, and Roxy's bedroom as a play-room. Now he had to share a room with Brian and move all of his toys to the basement. Brian was used to sharing a room with two other brothers, so he didn't mind rooming with Gold. Besides, he was the oldest and set the rules for the room. Gold could not adjust to this new lifestyle because for almost eight years he had been the only child. Roxy, Brian, and B.J were killing his plans of being mom's spoiled child. He had always thought it would be cool to have a brother or sister to play with, but this was definitely not what Gold had in mind.

While everyone was trying to adjust, B.J's imminent prison sentence had them all on ice because they did not know what the future held. When B.J went to his pre-trail hearing, his lawyer assured him it would take at least two months before his final trial date would be set, due to the complexity of the case. This meant more time for the family to worry about what they would do when he was gone. Sparkle worried about how she was going to support three kids and pay a four hundred and fifty dollar house note plus the other bills when B.J went away to prison. B.J was hoping he would not have to serve the full fifteen to life sentence that his crime demanded. Roxy and Brian were considering which family member they would go live with once their father left. They really did not have a problem with Sparkle, but the only reason they dealt with her was because of their father. Young Gold was the most relaxed about the situation. He just wanted everything to be over with so he and his mother could continue the new life they had started before B.J's invasion.

The time finally came: August 17, 1982, the final day of B.J's trial. Sparkle and B.J's mother sat nervously in the courtroom waiting for the judge to announce the sentence. The only sound present in the room was low level chatter. Then the pounding of the judge's gavel sounded loudly against the desk as he took a deep breath to gain attention. "After reviewing the evidence of this case, I sentence Brian J. Holes to six years in a maximum security prison," stated the judge. The reaction from B.J's family was more joyful than anyone in the courtroom expected. B.J was the most relieved of all. He had witnessed many of his friends lose touch with their family and friends because of long prison terms. If he had to serve the full fifteen years, he would have lost his life and everyone in it. Every since the trial began, B.J had feared of becoming one of those prisoners who felt dead inside due to loss of communication with family and friends. He figured with a fifteen-year sentence, Sparkle and his family would have hung in there for a few years. But when reality slapped them in the face, the letters and the visits would have come to an end.

Under the circumstances, six years was fine with B.J. He knew a lot would change by the time of his release. But he prayed that nothing would change drastically enough to separate him from his family and Sparkle. He also appreciated the judge granting him four weeks to turn himself in, due to his prompt appearances on scheduled court dates. This gave B.J a chance to spend more time with Sparkle and the new family they had pulled together. In those four weeks B.J and Sparkle spent a lot of time together while Roxy and Brian got the honor of staying home with Gold, or dragging him along with them if they wanted to go somewhere. Roxy, Brian, and Gold had burdens placed on their lives because of their selfish parents. Gold was use to having his own key to the house so he could come and go as he pleased. Roxy and Brian were use to living their teenage lives without having to baby-sit. It was hell from the beginning as far as the children were concerned. But they knew it wouldn't last for long because B.J would soon be gone. Without him there to dictate these straining rules, they would gain their freedom back. It was the moments when they were treated unfairly that made Young Gold's relationship with Roxy and Brian take a more brotherly and sisterly form.

About a month after B.J was gone, his wife came back from Texas. She had stayed in contact with Roxy and Brian while she and the other two children were away. When she arrived back in town she came to visit them one night. Roxy was out on a date with her boyfriend and Sparkle was at her mother's house. The boys were the only ones at home. Before she arrived that night, Brian had been on the phone begging her to come and get him. "I don't want to stay here anymore, I want to come live with you," he coaxed in a weak voice. Gold was listening to the telephone conversation as usual, so Brian yelled for him to get out of the room. Gold already knew what was going on, but Brian was afraid Gold would tell Sparkle, and that she wouldn't allow him to leave. Instead, Gold was glad things were working out this way. He even helped Brian pack and carry his stuff out to the car when his mom came.

By the time Brian and Roxy's mother arrived, Roxy was home. She asked Brian, "What are you doing? Dad is going to go off when he finds out you left with her!" The only two words Roxy spoke to her mother were hi and bye. She enjoyed the freedom she had with Sparkle, so there was no way she was leaving. Plus, she had promised her dad she would help Sparkle stay in his corner until he got home.

Sparkle wasn't the least bit bothered by Brian's decision to leave. She thought it was best for him to be with his mother so some of the pressure would be taken off her. Gold got his house key back, started having friends over to stay the night, and most importantly, got his mother back. Everything was not yet as Gold imagined his new living environment to be, but he was living like a seven-year-old adult again. Roxy was still there, but she was just like one of his mother's friends. Gold was so used to one of his mother's friends living or staying at their house for long periods of time, that Roxy wasn't a bother. And by the time she moved out, she and Gold had brotherly and sisterly love for one another. Gold did not want to see Roxy leave. She was always there to talk to him when his mother was getting on his nerves. But she was eighteen, had a nice boyfriend, and was ready to get her own life started, so she moved out. She stayed in touch with Gold, and on some weekends she did things with him that Great Big sisters do. His favorite was when she would take him to the shopping malls in Cincinnati to play in the game rooms. They always had the latest games. Even when she started having her own children, she still made time for Gold.

Chapter 5

Things were now somewhat back to normal in Young Gold's life. But the positive road he and his mother had started down a year ago had been blocked. Back when B.J's trial had begun, Sparkle had put all her energy into helping him instead of helping herself. While she was helping B.J fight his no-win armed robbery/murder case she took a leave from work that lasted six or seven months. She was so strung out on her relationship; she forgot what was best for her and Gold. B.J was going to the penitentiary whether or not she went to work. And by her failing to realize that fact, she found herself in a financial bind just a few months after he was gone. The bills were stacking up and someone else had filled her spot at the nursing home. She and B.J's mother had also stopped attending Mr. Smith's church services after the trial, which left him feeling, used. He felt they had only participated in his church for B.J's sake. Mr. Smith saw it as using him and the Lord, so he no longer provided jobs for Sparkle. Both of her financial providers turned their backs on her, just as she had turned her back on them to help B.J.

Sparkle was desperately searching for a way out, but her focus was gone. To get the tension off her mind she started to mingle with her friends again. One of the friends she used to work with at the nursing home became her new comrade. Chukka no longer worked at the nursing home either. She now worked for a private home care agency. She set her own schedule so there was plenty of time for her and Sparkle to hang out. It started out as a weekend thing that quickly grew into an everyday party when Chukka moved in with Sparkle and Gold.

It helped out financially, but it brought the high life back into their home. This time the aroma of marijuana joints that passed through the air was accompanied by the devil himself, Alcohol. Young Gold had known his mother to drink a little Remy Martin or other top shelf liquor during the holidays, but he did not understand what had her drinking six to twelve bottles or cans of beer a day. All of the things that once before held Sparkle back from fulfilling her dreams were on their way to hold her back a second time, and this time Alcohol was involved.

When the police raided Gold's and his mother's apartment that Friday night, he had no idea what white stuff they were looking for, but he did know what marijuana was. One Sunday, after Gold came home from his weekend stay at his grandma's, he found a plate under the couch with some white powdery stuff on it. He was not being meddle-some. One of his Hot Wheel cars just happened to roll underneath the couch while his mother was sitting there watching television. Gold asked, "Mom, is this the white stuff the police were looking for that night?" She tried to blow the question off by ignoring him, but Gold asked again, "What is this? What is it used for? How is it used, and why?" Gold really wanted to know about the white stuff on the plate because he still was having nightmares about the police wrecking their house looking for it. There was no way she was going to tell Gold the drugs belonged to her. To keep herself in the clear, Sparkle said the plate belonged to Chukka. Then she thought to herself for a minute about how she might explain what cocaine and drugs were to her eight-year-old son. Gold tried to sit there patiently, but he was so eager to know he continued to ask more questions as his mother sat there with her mind reeling. "Is it like the weed that you all be smoking?" he asked, waiting for an answer. She told him in terms that he could understand, "No, they are two different drugs." "What are drugs?" he asked. She started by explaining the two categories of drugs. "Uppers speed the body up, and downers slow the body down," she explained. Then she identified some of the different names that certain drugs were called and told him where they came from. She explained to him why people use cocaine, marijuana, and other drugs. "Different drugs give people certain feelings; some people like to speed, and others like to slow down and relax, but the main reason they use them are that they get hooked," she pointed out, clearing her throat. Now Gold wanted to know what drugs she had used before. After she finished telling him all the gruesome ways people put drugs into their bodies, he asked, "Mom, have you ever used that coke stuff before?" She responded, stuttering, "I tried it before, but it's not something that I'm hooked on." Finally, Gold understood what drugs were, how they were used, and the reasons people continued to use them, but he was still unclear why the police treated him and his mother the way they had that Friday night.

Sparkle knew it would be hard to sneak around the house using any type of drug, now that Gold knew all about them. So later that night when Chukka came home, Sparkle told her that Gold had found the plate under the couch. Gold had seen his mother and other people use drugs before without their knowing, but he hadn't known what they were doing. That next morning, Young Gold went to his mother to tell her that he loved her, and he did not want her to die from using drugs. He would always tell her, "The next puff might be your last." That day, all of the drug activity came to an end. Sparkle got back on the positive track that she had been on when she and Young Gold first moved.

Chukka helped Sparkle land a decent pay nurse's aide position with the same private home care agency she worked for. Sparkle started out with two patients, and a month later she had a total of four. Her weekly salary averaged close to forty-five dollars a patient, and Chukka paid her one hundred and fifty dollars each month to stay there. But even still, money for the monthly bills fell short. Sparkle had two choices. She could either work two jobs, or move out of the house. A second job would help her catch up on the bills and possibly get ahead. There was no way she could afford to move right then because she was too far in the hole. Plus Chukka was on the verge of moving out. It was killing her not to be able to get high in the house. Chukka felt since she paid bills, she was free to do, as she pleased. But Sparkle stressed to her that drug use in the house was disrespectful to Gold.

When Chukka moved out, the hundred and fifty dollars that fell out of Sparkle's monthly budget really made the situation worse. There was too much room in the house for Gold and Sparkle, and there wasn't enough money coming in to afford the house anymore. If Sparkle had never gotten behind, she could have easily afforded the house with the two incomes she was bringing in when she and Gold first moved.

Now that Chukka was gone, it was time for Sparkle to make some decisions. One of her private home care patients had also died at the time, so employment came first. She wanted to stay in the nursing field because that's what she was currently doing. At the time, high paying nursing positions were filled frequently, but there were two problems -- none of the high paying jobs were in the area where Sparkle lived, and they all required a certain amount of credit hours to have been earned from a qualified nursing school. The positive road Sparkle started out on when she first left home from her mother's stared her in the face. Sparkle finally had a fair chance to get her life together. She had a chance to put the ghetto street lifestyle behind her and Young Gold for good. This was the break that Sparkle had been looking for, and there was no way that she was going to let the opportunity pass her by.

Chapter 6

In 1983, all the modeling, sewing, bartending, interior decorating, and A-1 single parenting finally paid off. Through hard work and determination Sparkle went to nursing school and landed a good-paying job at Springtree Nursing Home on the south side of town. The nursing home was very cooperative. They allowed Sparkle to work while she finished her last three months of school, but she had to let her home care patients go. It was not a problem for her, the street life she had recently left behind taught her all about sacrifice. After all, when she finished nursing school, her current salary plus the income from her three home care patients would not compare to her new salary at Springtree. It all worked out perfectly. Within the first three months Sparkle gained a tremendous amount of love for her new job, and began to grow close to the patients there. They loved to see her warm and pretty smile everyday. It brought their spirits up. Some families even took their loved ones out of Springtree and paid Sparkle to care for them at home. The money she sacrificed in the beginning came back to her in the end. Gold was very proud of his mother. She was working again, not using drugs as far as he knew, and trying to build a future for them.

All of the house bills were finally caught up. Sparkle even had a little money put aside. She was ready for a real change, and the long drive to work was becoming a real hassle. Everything was coming together so perfectly she felt it was time to start working on the educational dreams she had for Gold. He was in the second grade and had been held back a year because of his reading. School was nearly out for the summer, but she enrolled him in summer school to see if he was really having problems in reading, or if he was having problems with the way it was being taught. It also allowed her more free time to work.

At the end of Young Gold's summer school classes he was reading at his correct grade level, though he only earned a "C" in the class. Sparkle concluded it was the school system having teaching problems, not Gold learning. So, with the money she had saved, and the extra income from her home care patients, she decided to move closer to work and to a better educational environment for Young Gold. With him just being eight, Sparkle hoped that a new environment would help heal some of the scars stuck in his mind from the traumatic events he had to face throughout the first seven years of his life.

Littleton was a suburban town about twenty miles outside of the inner city. The town was mostly populated with middle and upper class whites. Young Gold quickly realized that his new environment was different indeed. The people in the neighborhood were very close and respectful to each other. They were not stealing, fighting, and killing one another over parking spaces and loose change for drugs or alcohol. Instead, the people in Littleton were calm, understanding, and giving. People in the stores, schools, gas stations, and streets were polite and considerate. And while Gold's apartment complex in Littleton was filled with families of different races, mostly white, everyone lived like one big extended family.

Gold wasn't bothered by the fact that he was a minority in the apartment complex. His mother taught him to judge people by the way they treated him, and not to be prejudiced or biased. During the first two months of the year, Young Gold enjoyed celebrating Martin Luther

King, JR's birthday and Black History Month with his mother. She told him stories about slavery, the civil rights movement, and the marches that Doctor King led, trying to bring white and black people together. She even told him how good it felt to participate in marches that Doctor King led. She often explained, "I felt good inside participating in civil rights events because I was marching or speaking up to gain recognition for all people to come together". This made Gold feel secure when he communicated with the white children in his neighborhood. He did not focus on their race. He judged people as individuals. Most of the white people he met judged him the same way. He realized that the saying 'Treat others like you want to be treated' was true, and Gold lived by it in every environment he entered.

All of Gold's family worried about him and Sparkle because they lived so far out, with so many white people. They feared some crazed racist would attack Gold going to, or coming home from school one day. They called often to check on them, but rarely visited, complaining that the drive was to far. Gold never experienced any racial confrontations there, but Sparkle did. One day she went to pay a speeding ticket in Clarksburg, a town neighboring Littleton. She had no idea where the Clarksburg courthouse was located, so she stopped at a 7-Eleven convenience store for directions. When she came out of the store, four white teenagers threw rocks at her car and yelled, "you, nigger, get out of here" as she pulled off. When she got to the courthouse she reported the incident to the police, but they never caught the boys Sparkle described. When Young Gold's Grandma April found out about Sparkle's incident, she insisted Gold stay with her for the rest of the summer, afraid something like that might happen to him with the neighborhood children. Gold was only used to being around children in the family and she worried about how well he would adjust and make new friends where they lived now. Sparkle's racial encounter made her feel even worse. April was always worried about her grandchildren, especially Gold because he was her first.

Gold refused to leave Littleton for the summer. Finally, he was living the life he had always dreamed of. There were wooded bike trails for him to ride on, an area in the woods designated for shooting pellet guns, two swimming pools, a basketball court, and four nets for tennis - all located inside the apartment complex. Friends were Gold's least worry. His grandma's mind still was not at ease. So, to make her feel more secure, Gold visited her house on weekends. And Sparkle allowed Rachel's two children, Dee and Joe Joe, to visit during the week since school was out. Young Gold was having his best summer ever, but it was soon time for school, and he had to get down to business.

Gold loved his new neighborhood, so he was very excited about starting his new school. He was a little jittery because his friend Jason from the apartment complex went to a different school in the district. Gold had hoped Jason would show him around school and introduce him to all the cool kids just like he had done when Gold first moved into the apartment complex.

Gold's first day of school at Roland Shade Elementary came. The name made him feel at home because it kind of reminded him of his own name, Roland Che'. When he walked into his third grade classroom, he was completely amazed. There was a male teacher, and all of the students were white -- two scenarios he had never imagined. The teacher, Mr. Wilkey, and the students pleasantly welcomed Gold into the class. It was just as new of an experience for them as it was for Gold, because he was the only black student in the entire school. They all looked past his brown skin and into his warm colored soul. He was treated no differently from any other student in the classroom.

All of the special attention Gold received from his peers motivated him to learn and excel just as they did. He felt like an exchange student who everyone wanted to be around, and learn about. His first report card from Roland Shade was filled with O's for outstanding. Sparkle was proud. She now felt she could loosen up a little and give Gold more control of his life. From that point on there was no holding Gold back from getting his education. He fell in love with school because; unlike at his previous schools, here he learned something new every day. This was how Sparkle always wanted their lives to be. But without a positive man in their lives, or Gold's father, she had to conquer devious obstacles that stood in her way.

Chapter 7

A year and an half after Sparkle and Gold moved to Littleton, Sparkle ran into one of her old friends from Mason who used to sell women's clothing, purses, and dress shoes. She hadn't seen him in several years. She first asked him about his business. She thought about maybe upgrading her wardrobe now that she could afford to. Jay sold only top of the line women's fashion products. But over the years he had upgraded his products to still a higher level. He no longer dealt in women's clothing, purses, and dress shoes. Jay was now into big time drug dealing with some men from down south. Sparkle could not believe what she was hearing because when she last saw him, he was a very successful businessman, so she had thought. But she remembered that she had originally met him though B.J.

A few weekends later Jay and three of his friends stopped by Sparkle's house. One of them was from Ft. Lauderdale, Florida, near an area where Sparkle had other friends. So they talked about the area and the names of different people who lived there to see if they shared acquaintances, and one conversation led to another. Jay sat there pretending to be interested, but he could not hide his jealousy. He was extremely bothered by Sparkle and Bone exchanging phone numbers before they left. Jay planned on asking Sparkle to hook him up with some people in the city who might want to buy large quantities of his supplies. He feared that if Bone got close to Sparkle, he might be cut out.

About a month later, Bone and his two nephews, Kid and Skip, came to town. On the Saturday that they were leaving to go home, they stopped by Sparkle's to visit for awhile. As a gift, Bone gave her a set of nice, tan leather luggage with combination locks on the two biggest suitcases. That Sunday night, after Sparkle picked Young Gold up from her mother's house, they came home to find their apartment had been broken into. The closets were wrecked and clothes were scattered everywhere. The neighbors across the hall claimed to have seen a tall black man with short curly hair entering the apartment about 10:15 p.m., just forty-five minutes before Gold and Sparkle got home. Nothing in the apartment was missing, and the only things damaged besides the door were the two locked suitcases. From the neighbor's description of the man they had seen, Sparkle was convinced the burglar was Jay.

Earlier that Saturday, when Bone and his nephews had come to Sparkle's house, Jay had been watching from across the parking lot. He thought Bone was carrying drugs or money in the luggage he had carried into the house, but the suitcases were empty. Bone had already taken care of his business and didn't have room for the luggage, so he had given it to Sparkle. The day after the break-in, Sparkle called Bone to inform him of what had happened. "I don't think you should trust Jay; he may have broken into my apartment last night," she warned. "Were you hurt? Are you all right? Is anything missing?" Bone inquired, concerned. When she told him the two suitcases were cut, he knew right away that Jay had something to do with the break-in. Bone told her that Jay provided him with all of the luggage that he used. And since the luggage was the only thing tampered with, all fingers pointed to Jay. So the following weekend, Bone and his two nephews came to town to handle the situation and Jay never surfaced again.

The loyalty that Sparkle and Bone showed towards each other in handling the Jay situation, despite their short acquaintance, quickly formed them into good friends. Kid and Skip became someone who Gold looked up to, like big brothers, or older cousins. Now, instead of staying in hotels when they came to town, they sometimes stayed with Gold and Sparkle. Bone would pay the whole phone bill when he came because he used the line for a lot of long distance calls. And he would give Sparkle two or three hundred dollars to put in her pocket for letting them stay at her house. But after the incident with Jay, Sparkle told Bone about what she had gone through with Silver, the police raid, and all the drama from the streets. "I just got away from that life, and I don't want to take Gold back down that road," she insisted. She did not care what Bone was into. She was just trying to make it clear that she didn't want any illegal business around her home. She had to be concerned with Gold's safety. Bone respected her wishes because he had two children of his own and understood how she felt. She was overwhelmingly impressed with Bone, and his financial status was another plus. Within only six months of knowing him she began to discuss marriage.

In February of 1984, Sparkle and Bone exchanged vows at the courthouse in Littleton. There were no chiming church bells, bright lights, or rows of seats filled with friends and family. It was just him, her, and her mother. Young Gold wanted no part of the wedding. He felt his mother was rushing into a lifetime relationship with a man she knew nothing about. He also did not like the fact that the bonding time with his mother would be shortened again. She had another man in her life, and the little time she had away from work would now be spent with her husband instead of with Gold.

It took about three months for Bone and Sparkle to settle into their marriage and their new home. They moved into a luxury townhouse inside the complex that Sparkle currently lived in. The rent was one hundred dollars more a month than the apartment Gold and Sparkle had lived in before. The newlyweds could easily afford the rent payment with both of them bringing in high incomes. Sparkle was back into her nursing, Bone continued traveling, taking care of his business, and Gold was stuck trying to figure out why his mother was attempting to spend the rest of her life with this man. The whole marriage was a mess. Gold had become accustomed to the smooth road he and his mother traveled alone. Gold already recognized that whenever his mother brought a man from the outside into the family, it caused a problem. Sparkle was calling on a mechanic to balance the tires when the road was the real problem.

It was hard for Young Gold to get into Bone. He never had much to converse about with Gold, which made him feel like Bone was hiding something. And it did not take long for Bone's true colors to come into focus. After Sparkle introduced him to some of her friends from the streets, the shit hit the fan. Bone started bringing his business home instead of taking care of it out of town like he used to. He thought since he was the man of the house, and the people he dealt with were ex-friends of his wife, there was no problem. Bone no longer respected Sparkle's feelings about drugs in her home and around her son. The talk she had with him when they first met about her having already lived that life and not wanting to repeat it, was lost in his memory. She just wanted to continue working her two nursing jobs so Gold could grow, learn, and excel in a nice environment where there was very little drug and violent activity.

The hidden side of Bone revealed itself. Sparkle did not expect her marriage to last for a short seven or eight months. In the beginning, she knew Bone was into illegal business and that he had been to prison for murder, but she did not know that a troublesome cocaine habit came with his lifestyle and money. The risk Sparkle took was almost life taking.

Chapter 8

The night before Bone let his true identity shine, Gold laid in bed worried about his mother because she had not come home yet. All that month Bone had badly verbally abused Sparkle, so Gold knew there were problems in their relationship. The words Gold heard Bone say to his mother tore his nine-year-old heart to pieces. Just by the way Bone yelled at Sparkle, Gold thought he was going to kill her. When Young Gold woke up the next morning and found his mother still wasn't home, he headed to ask Bone but stopped when the phone rang. Gold picked it up, but stayed silent on the line, listening. Bone started yelling and screaming. It was Sparkle on the line. Gold wanted to say something to his mother, but knew if he stayed quiet and listened to the conversation he would find out what was going on. Gold heard Bone say, "If you don't bring me my dope, I'm not letting your son go to school." Right after Bone hung up the phone, Gold quickly dressed himself and left the house headed to his friend Jason's to call his mother to tell her he was safe. It was too late. She had already left to come home to save him. Bone knew how she felt about Gold and that she would come home. She'd rather give her life than have anything happen to her child.

When Young Gold got home from school that day, Bone had taken an aluminum baseball bat to Sparkle's head and a knife to the back of her neck, leaving her with a badly bruised skull and a cut that took fourteen stitches. A young white couple who lived across the street came rushing to Sparkle's aid when they saw the flashing lights of the paramedics and the police cars. With the little strength she had left in her body she muttered, "Please watch for my son and give him this number to call, as she handed a note to the lady." Gold got off the school bus at 3:15 p.m. and Angel was in her window watching for him. She yelled his name and hurried to meet him in the middle of the street with the note as he got off the school bus. It said to call his grandma's house right away. Angel didn't mention anything to him about what had happened to his mother. But as they parted, she told him to knock on her door if he needed anything. Even though Young Gold did not know Angel, he sensed something was wrong by the way that she was acting. And normally, when his mother had a note for him, she would leave it on the table close to the front door. He thought about the conversation between his mother and Bone earlier that morning. It had been the only thing on his mind all day at school. And now that neither Bone nor his mother were home, he went in the house looking for clues as to what might have happened after he left for school and why one of the neighbors had given him a note.

Gold unlocked the door and opened it slowly. He expected to see blood everywhere, or the house torn up. He searched the upstairs first, then came back down to find nothing but a quiet house, so he called his grandma. She told him she was going to send his Aunt Rachel after him. Before he could ask where his mother was, she said she would talk to him when he arrived. Gold was a nervous wreck during the drive to his grandma's. With the conversation he heard before school, he didn't know if his mother was kidnapped, in the hospital, or dead. When he got to his grandma's house, everyone seemed to be worried. Everyone in the family was there, everyone but his mother. He knew it had something to do with her. He also knew it was something severe, because his Aunt Rachel was driving his mother's car.

Gold went into the bathroom and started to cry. He knew something had happened to his mother. While he was blowing his nose, trying to stop tears from running down his face, he heard the phone ring. He ran into the kitchen to get it, but his grandmother was already talking. It was Sparkle. She was ready for someone to pick her up from the hospital. "Is Gold there?" she asked. "Yes," her mother replied. Gold's Grandma April handed him the phone. Sparkle asked, " Are you all right? Did he do anything to you?" "No. After I heard you all talking on the phone this morning I got dressed and ran to Jason's house to call you, but you were gone," Gold replied in between breaths as he tried to stop crying. She told him that, "if you weren't there, I would not have come home. I just wanted to make sure you were safe."

It took Sparkle about two weeks to recover from the brutal attack, but she marched through it like a true soldier. The police did not do anything to Bone because Sparkle was his wife. At the time, domestic violence laws were not strict. But the attack ended their relationship. Bone moved to South Carolina to live with his sister, and Sparkle never heard from him again.

Chapter 9

Sparkle and Gold struggled after she and Bone split up. She was in a financial situation similar to when B.J left. She was doing everything in her power to keep the rent and the bills paid. She worked longer hours on both jobs, borrowed money when she needed, and even tried to contact Bone for some money. The fact that again she had let a man come into her and Gold's lives and pull them down killed her inside. She held on for as long as she could, but that fourth month took her under. The rent payment was the major bill and it gave her the most trouble. She could not get it paid on time. The rental office enforced a seventy-five dollar late fee policy, and Sparkle was two weeks late on every payment after Bone left. That extra seventy-five dollars a month quickly forced her to start looking for more affordable housing. It became extremely difficult for her to keep the bills up, and raise Gold at the same time. Gold's father was not in their lives, nor was her father. The only person they could turn to was her mother, but things were not peaches and cream for her either.

Grandma April had been working on a hit song with one of her business partners. He was a talented musician who was working with some of the top R&B artists in the music industry. Then he let drugs turn him into one of the snakes of the entertainment world. He got caught up in the high life of the business. To support his drug habit he stole the song he and April were working on, and sold it to one of the biggest recording companies in the city. He received a lump of twenty-five thousand-dollar advancement payment, while April and her family received nothing but sorrow. During the first week the song hit the air, April received phone calls from all of her friends, "Girl, your song is on the radio!" they all chanted, amazed. Even family members were calling in an uproar, "I heard the song on the radio! We're rich! We're rich!" April and her family were most definitely supposed to be rich, because two weeks later her song was at the top of the charts. After all of April's friends and family came down off their high horses, in agony and pain she told them her million-dollar song had been stolen from her. When Gold would hear her song on the radio he would brag to his friends, "My grandmother wrote that song." They never believed him. They would say, "If she wrote it, why aren't you rich?" Gold could not answer that question. He could not understand why he wasn't rich until he got older and understood what had happened.

April traveled from city to city, paying lawyers, trying to get the rights to her song. Because of the legal and traveling expenses she had to pay, her financial status was at a minimum. She was in the process of losing her dream house, and her chance of winning the case was not promising. When things were really at rock bottom for Gold and his family, another man came into their lives, but he was quite different from the others. He was like an angel sent from up above to rescue Gold and his family.

A few weeks before April's day in court, her friend Marsha took her to a man that lived on the north side of Dayton in a low-income apartment complex named Crestmore. Marsha and other friends of April were trying to do everything they could to help her break the depression she was going though. Marsha thought some company from a kind freehearted man was what she needed.

The OLE Man and April kicked things off overnight. He filled the shoes so many other men had left behind. He helped her in every way he possibly could. He noticed from day one that something was troubling her. He commented one day, "You're too pretty to be looking all sad and depressed. If you were my lady friend, I would keep you smiling." The day April and her friend Marsha were at the OLE Man's house, he gave her his phone number and said, "Call me if you need anything, or someone to talk to." The whole ride home Marsha told April, "You better get with him, he likes you, and he got it going on." April laughed to herself, "How can a man living in some low-income apartment help me." But when April and her family had their backs against the wall, the OLE Man helped relieve the pressure.

Later that week, April called the OLE Man and asked, "Do you mind stopping past my house when you get a chance?" When he arrived, they ate dinner and she explained to him the financial problems she was having due to the money she spent trying to win the rights to her song. He asked, "Can I do anything to help?" She really did not want to put her burden on him, but she desperately needed mental, emotional, and financial support. "I need a way to get back and forth to Chicago, to get things squared away with my lawyer before we go to court, but my biggest problem is that I have less than thirty days to move out of my home," she admitted sadly.

At the time, the OLE Man sold cars for one of his gambling buddy's who owned a dealership. His friend would give the OLE Man two or three cars to drive around in to sell them. There was a brand new 1986 Ford LTD that came in, and later that day, when April came home it was parked in her driveway. She left for Chicago two days later. And when she came back from her second trip, the OLE Man gave her keys and deed papers to a new house, which was just around the corner from the home she had lost. He had also offered to help Sparkle get a low-income townhouse in Crestmore. The OLE Man treated April and her family like they were his own.

A week before April's court hearing against her business partners, she received a phone call from her lawyer in Chicago. They had offered her fifteen thousand to settle. She turned the money down, which led to her and the OLE Man's first, and biggest fight. "You are a damn fool for not taking that money!" he screamed. "I'm not giving them my song! They are already making thousands off of it!" she screamed back. The OLE Man left, shaking his head, "You'll see."

A week later April got her day in court, and the judge came to a decision. April was looked at and laughed at as if she was nobody, when in reality she was the mastermind of the song which was well on its way to producing millions of dollars. Young Gold's and his family's pretty green grass was slowly turning brown, and their fortress was caving in. At ten, he could see his dreams of going to college and becoming someone famous, vanishing.

While Sparkle and Gold were preparing to move, the young newly-wed couple across the street that had come to Sparkle's rescue that day, became concerned neighbors and caring friends. One weekend Angel and Ross had company in from out of town, a man name Stoney from Trinidad. He wanted to meet a nice lady while he was in town and Angel and Ross had the right lady for him -- Sparkle. They knew she was having problems ever since the incident with Bone, and they thought a nice dinner with friends might help a little. That Saturday night Sparkle and Gold went to Ross and Angel's house for dinner. When Stoney introduced himself, Gold broke out in laughter because of

Stoney's accent. That was the first time Gold had ever met someone from another country. Gold really got a kick out of hearing Stoney talk. Sparkle thought he was being rude, so after dinner she sent him upstairs to play with Ross and Angel's two boys, Scott and Greg. Scott was three, and Greg was five, so Gold felt as if he was playing baby-sitter. During the last two months that Gold and his mother lived in Littleton, they grew extremely close to Angel and Ross.

Bone was no longer around to watch Gold while Sparkle worked her third-shift job at the nursing home. So, Angel and Ross allowed Gold to stay at their house free of charge while she worked. Gold fit in like their third child. When their friends visited, they would always ask, "Who is that little black kid?" And Angel and Ross would answer, "That's our other son." All of Scott and Greg's friends asked, "Why do you have a black brother?" They would respond, "To beat you up." They loved Gold so much that Angel asked Sparkle if they could adopt him. It surprised her. She was proud Angel and Ross felt that way about her son, but adoption was out of the question.

There were only two grading periods left in the school year when Gold and Sparkle moved. Angel begged Sparkle to let Gold finish the school year in Littleton from her house. But Sparkle saw no sense in him staying in the Littleton school district. She argued, "Sooner or later, he is going to have to get used to his new neighborhood and his new school, whether he likes it or not." She wasn't trying to be nasty about the decision she had made, so she allowed Angel and Ross to get Gold on the weekends.

Gold's grandmother, April, did not understand why Sparkle allowed Gold to stay with Angel and Ross. She always had a certain prejudice towards white people because they were often in the media for child molestation and things of that nature. Ross's family was very high class. They looked down on blacks and people in the lower social classes, and wondered why Angel and Ross wanted Gold around their family. But Angel's parents understood the feelings Angel and Ross had for Gold and welcomed him into their home, showing him the same type of love that Angel and Ross showed him. And when Scott and Greg started referring to Gold as their brother, and Gold started to refer to Angel and Ross as his parents, everyone from both families knew the feelings expressed between them were real.

Gold was not taking away any love from his mother, but Angel and Ross were the two parents Gold always wished he had. Whenever he needed someone to talk to, Angel took the time to listen. She and Ross saw lots of potential in him, and they did not want to see it ruined by the environment he was moving to. As a teenager, Ross grew up around some of the trash in poverty neighborhoods. He had witnessed the activities of druggies and drunks in those communities, making it hard for kids like Gold to see the positive things life had to offer. That's why they wanted Gold to stay with them. Then they realized it would not be too bad if he continued to focus on his education as he had done in Littleton. And during his free time on weekends they would have him.

Not long after the OLE Man got Sparkle into Crestmore she had to quit both of her nursing home jobs, so she only worked part-time caring for her home care patients. The rent in Crestmore was based on one's income. With her original income she would have had to pay over three hundred dollars a month. She refused to pay that when her neighbors were paying from two to fifty dollars a month. The OLE Man knew this meant she would have too much free time on her hands, and he did not want to see her get caught up and taken under by the ghetto environment. He kept her motivated and eager, and tried to show her how the projects could be used as a stepping stone to obtain the finer things in life for herself and Gold. He stressed, "It's not always about where you live, but how you live, and what you are doing to progress your social status."

The first time Sparkle took Gold to Crestmore to see their new apartment he was filled with disgust. There was no carpet on the floors, no dishwasher, no washer/dryer, no tennis courts or swimming pool, nothing that they had in Littleton. He got slapped across the face for carrying on about how he was not going to live there. "I'll stay with Granny, or Angel and Ross. I don't want to live here!" he cried. From the looks of the apartment, Gold did not want to imagine the character of the neighborhood or the children he would have to play with.

It was not until the first day at his new school that he met any kids from the neighborhood. When he stepped into the classroom he took a quick survey. There were two blacks -- three including himself -- one Latino, and all the rest were white. He thought to himself, "It might not be that bad." But that evening when he got home from school, his new friend Bryan, from his class, showed him around the neighborhood. It was certainly different from Littleton. Most of the boys his age spent their time stealing from the local drug and grocery stores, across the street from the complex, to eat, buy clothing, or help their family pay bills. And there were girls as young as twelve years old prostituting and performing oral sex for meals and money. Most of the adults who lived there didn't want much out of life for themselves or for their children.

Gold's white friends from school would visit and comment on how nice his apartment was. His peers from school and the complex thought he and Sparkle were rich and would often ask, "Why do you live here with the drugs and violence?" Gold did not know at the time, but the OLE Man was the reason they lived in Crestmore. The OLE Man inspired Sparkle because he lived in the projects by choice, and still managed to obtain the finer things in life for himself and his family. He had a nice apartment, drove nice cars, and wore a different suit every day. He was the only person in the complex she could relate to. In the two and a half years they spent as neighbors, they grew very close. Sparkle and Gold felt like he took the place of the grandfathers, fathers, uncles, and brothers who were absent from their lives, and it had nothing to do with the OLE Man being involved with April. He treated Sparkle like a long lost daughter he had just found in distress. And in those two and a half years, the OLE Man kept Sparkle strong and striving to achieve the educational goals she had set for Gold. He kept her going, and she kept Gold going, because the first year in Crestmore, Gold felt like he was in his last years of life.

Chapter 10

The other children in Crestmore did not like him because his lifestyle was much different than theirs. He was not into fighting, stealing, and causing trouble. Plus he was a spoiled child. He had the expensive clothes, toys, and bikes they did not have. They assumed Gold thought he was better than they were. So, instead of being where he was not liked, that whole first year they lived in Crestmore he went to his grandmother's after school and to Angel and Ross's house on the weekends. The following year Gold entered junior high school, and got involved in as many extra curricular activities as he could. He played a sport every season and was the treasurer of the student council all three years. He figured the more time he spent at school, the less time he had to spend in the projects. This also meant there was less time for him to spend with his grandmother, and Angel and Ross. They were not heartbroken. They understood he was getting older, and knew how much he loved to be involved in school activities, so they gave him their support.

By the time Gold reached high school, he tried to avoid both the projects and his home life because his mother had begun to go backwards. And this time it wasn't going to be as easy as before for Sparkle to bounce back because negativity surrounded her. All the drugs, addicts, and street criteria were at her finger tips. The OLE Man had moved from Crestmore and his positive male guidance was gone. Gold was doing everything he could to see that things worked out for him and his mother. He was fifteen, starting his sophomore year in high school and felt like he was the man of the house and of the family. No other man in the family tried to step up to become a leader or a role model, so he gave it a shot. With him only being fifteen, he had to take a simple but intellectual approach to getting his family to recognize his leadership ability. Gold thought that if he excelled in school he would win them over. He knew his mother wanted him to excel in high school and then go to college because she had not been able to finish her own college education. Studying, working, and single parenting simultaneously had been too difficult for her, but Gold convinced himself he would pick up where she had left off.

There was nothing that could stop Gold from getting his education. His perfect attendance from the fourth grade on showed he was trying to be all he could be. In high school, it seemed as if he was a machine. He was class treasurer, lettered in cross-country and in track all four years, lettered in basketball two years, and held 'Scholar Athlete' status three out of four years in all three sports. He had the honor of taking center stage to be crowned 'All-Sports King' his sophomore and senior years. This stemmed from him becoming the first student in the school's history to make the All-Ohio Cross-country Team, winning conference while setting a new school record, and placing in the top ten in every meet in which he took part. The crowning received his senior year came from all-around achievements in basketball, cross-country, and track during his junior and senior years. Gold was team-captain and second team All-Conference in basketball, All-Conference and All-District in cross-country, and All-State in track. He got visits, phone calls, and letters from Division I Colleges throughout his high school career. He made school an enjoyable place for his teachers and for his peers. But no one truly understood where Gold got so much energy.

It was unusual for black students like Gold in a white school district to take advantage of the excellent education and opportunities offered to white students. Most of the black students who attended Gold's high school did not have the discipline and attitude it took to excel in a school environment where their color was the minority. With the tone he set throughout high school, black students in his class were more productive than in any previous class.

Young Gold made his mother feel like a celebrity when she called or visited the school for his Sports and Academic Award banquets. The director of the banquet would ask the parents to stand when their child came on stage to receive his or her award. Sparkle would stand in the spotlight the entire night. Her elegant dress and beautiful smile made it easy for other parents to recognize who her child was. But it would have been impossible for them to believe that Gold's accomplishments and commitment were fueled by his mother's horrendous lifestyle. During his sophomore year, when Sparkle fell back into the streets, school became a source of comfort to Gold, helping to heal the pain that home brought upon him. He knew the more he excelled in sports and academics, the less time he had to deal with life at home, then, and in the future.

Chapter 11

By the end of Young Gold's sophomore year at school, Sparkle's world had spun completely out of control. Just when Gold thought he had found a way to deal with the projects and fix his home life, his mother let B.J back into their lives. Three years had passed without any communication between the two. After she married Bone, B.J stopped writing and calling because he felt betrayed. He had expected her to wait the six years to be with him. She always felt guilty about not waiting, but she had to break away and better her life.

The day B.J was released from prison he went to Sparkle's grandmother's house. "Will you call Sparkle's for me?" he asked. There wasn't a man in Sparkle's life when B.J was released, so she was glad to hear from him. She gave him her address and told him it was fine for him to come over. When he got to Sparkle's apartment they hugged and kissed for at least thirty minutes, telling each other how much they had missed one another. Sparkle was lonely and back into the drugs, so it was easy for B.J to use her guilt and her weakness to get back into her life.

Gold could not believe that just as he was entering the most important years of his life, all of the burdens that had brought him and his mother down were back. B.J moving in, on top of Sparkle's lifestyle, was the worst thing that could possibly have happened to Young Gold. He thought his days of dealing with B.J were over, but they were just getting started. Not long after Sparkle and B.J got back together, she became pregnant. B.J wasted no time picking up where he had left off six years ago with Sparkle, and with his life in the streets.

Thanks to the six years in prison he had gained a lot more knowledge about the streets and how to get faster money. Most of the criminals he had met in prison were locked up for involvement in counterfeiting, heroin distribution, and murder for hire. So when he got back with Sparkle, he put all his knowledge together and started an operation that brought in big bucks.

In less than a year, B.J had stacked a hundred thousand dollars without any heat or encounters with the law. He brought in over five thousand dollars a day with the help of Sparkle and two other guys. Young Gold would count thousands of dollars each night after he finished his homework. For him, it was first-hand experience in accounting and economics. He loved to count money, and to get paid for it made him love it all the more. In one year's time Gold saved close to eight thousand dollars for himself. And it helped ease the harsh feelings he had for B.J, but it did not completely make him forget B.J's past treatment of his mother. Gold decided if his mother had to take the heat for B.J this time, he better prepare himself in advance. He knew the money, happiness, and laughs were not going to last forever because B.J was still going to be B.J. So every night, Gold would stash an extra fifty dollars away with the fifty B.J gave him for counting the money.

It was like Gold read the future because soon the money and all the happiness took a 180-degree turn for the worst. B.J lived the big time drug dealer life, and when he broke the rules he had to pay the big time drug dealer price. He started using his own product, which in his line of business was the one rule not to break. Many dealers advised, "Don't get high off your own supply." But B.J caught a taste of his own medicine, which happened to be the most addictive drug on the street.

The heroin ruined his attitude and made him greedy. He came to be on bad terms with local heroin dealers in the city because he took all the business. He was dealing with one of the top heroin suppliers in the city. And when his heroin supplier turned himself into a rehabilitation center, B.J bought him out. B.J quickly gained a majority of the city's clientele by only selling to addicts. This way, he could be the only big time dealer making money. But when he ran out of heroin, he had to go outside the city limits to purchase more because local dealers wouldn't deal with him.

After B.J had his successful run, he went through a three months' drought with no major supplier. A guy named Mark, who worked for him, knew some heroin dealers in Chicago and was in the process of setting up a deal. But during the three months without a steady supplier, B.J's finances had dropped from a hundred thousand dollars, to forty thousand dollars. His new high-class lifestyle and heroin habit drained him. He was not purchasing enough heroin to support his habit, live like the rich and famous, and keep his profits increasing or steady. Between B.J and his workers a quarter of an ounce of heroin was used within a week to support their own habits. At the wholesale price this equaled to seventeen hundred dollars worth of heroin. He was lucky that Mark finally got everything squared away with his buddies in Chicago before he went completely under.

The following Thursday after Mark set things up for B.J, they were to fly to Chicago. B.J thought it would be safest to fly out during the week because of tough airport security on the weekends. When Gold came home from basketball practice that afternoon, there was a note for him to set aside eighteen thousand dollars at the bottom of the safe. The money was in thin thousand dollar stacks, but Young Gold had to go through all eighteen to make sure the amount was correct. When B.J and Sparkle came home, Gold's job was done. All B.J had to do was safely pack the money in his luggage. The plane was scheduled to leave at 7:55 that night and B.J and Mark arrived at the airport about an hour ahead of time. They checked-in their bags and proceeded to step through the metal detectors when two groups of detectives grabbed them. "Come with us," one of the suited men demanded as they escorted B.J and Mark into rooms opposite of each other. Neither of them knew what was going on until the detectives placed them in the rooms and asked, "What's the sixteen thousand dollars going to be used for?" Mark told them he did not know anything about the money. They knew he was lying, but they let him go because it was not in his luggage. When they asked B.J the same question he told them he was in the process of starting his own pest control business and that he planned to purchase equipment. The detectives did not buy B.J's story either. "When you can show us proof of where the money came from, call this number and ask for me," the head detective stated. Then they let him go, and gave him a receipt showing the amount of money they had confiscated.

B.J and Mark took a cab back to Mark's house. From there B.J called Sparkle and told her what had happened. "Why didn't you come on home?" she asked. "I'm trying to get in touch with someone who can claim my damn money. I'll see you soon," he responded, sounding like someone gone mad. After the incident at the airport B.J's nerves were shot. He went back to Marks's house instead of going home so he could get a heroin fix. The detectives hadn't found the fourteen hundred dollars he had in his pocket. They only confiscated the money they saw on the X-ray monitor when B.J ran his bags through the machine. He could show the detectives proof of his plans to start a pest control business because he had completed classes in that field when he first came home from prison. But that did not prove the money came from a legal operation.

All that weekend B.J sat around the apartment with a tray full of heroin, powdering his nose. It was not until Wednesday that he was sober enough to contact friends and family to ask if they would claim his money for him. Everyone knew the money was drug related and refused to take the heat for him. His lawyer advised him to let the police keep the money or find a new occupation, because now they would watch him until a case was built against him. All his family and friends felt the same way. He lay low for about three more months, and those months drained the rest of his bank account and his life. The drug had made him thousands of dollars and brought drama to his life and to everyone's lives around him. He stayed in the house with his gold tray, loading his nose with brown dust. His substance abuse slowly but surely disintegrated the world Sparkle and Gold had lived in.

Gold thought B.J was going through some type of depression over losing the money at the airport, but it was the heroin taking a toll on his mind, body, and soul. His heroin habit was like a sickness. Some mornings he couldn't get out of bed until he had the drug in his system. Gold wondered why B.J didn't use the money he had left and start over. He wasn't totally broke. There were still about four thousand dollars in the safe, and a thousand dollars in his and Sparkle's unborn baby's bank. An ounce of heroin only cost about thirty-five hundred dollars. Young Gold's fifteen-year-old mind saw only how easy B.J had made the hundred thousand dollars. He couldn't comprehend the power the drug had to make people spend a hundred thousand dollars.

B.J's heroin addiction had become unbearable by the last grading period of Gold's sophomore year. Two or three nights out of a week Young Gold was awakened by yelling and screaming. "Bitch, give me my shit! I know you got it!" B.J yelled over and over again at the top of his lungs. One night Gold heard his mother calling his name as she gasped for air, "Gold, help! He's trying to kill me!" Gold jumped out of bed as fast as he could and ran into her bedroom. When he burst through the door B.J was on top of her with his hands around her neck. Gold was stunned for a moment. His mind flashing back to when he was six years old and first saw B.J hit his mother. Finally, Gold pushed him off her. B.J tried to kill Sparkle because he couldn't find his heroin. He thought she had taken it, but in reality he had used it all earlier that night. The heroin had B.J losing his mind. Occasionally, he even went to the extreme of accusing Gold of stealing his drugs. If he heard Gold blow into the tapes of his video games to clean them, he'd rush into the room expecting to catch Gold sniffing heroin. There were many mornings when Gold laid in bed thinking about killing his mother and B.J for bringing such stress and pain to his life. It was worse on the mornings after B.J had acted like a lunatic, and then carried on as if nothing had happened. Once he got high he was back to his normal happy self. Gold could not understand or deal with B.J's attitude and mood swings. One evening while B.J was away, Gold asked his mother why B.J's attitude changed so drastically, and why she continued to accept him. Sparkle had talked to Gold about marijuana and cocaine when he was younger, but she never expected to explain heroin to him. She first explained to him the addiction of the drug: "When it gets into your body, it makes you feel good and relaxed, like some type of strong pain medicine used by a doctor before an operation. And when the drug is out of your system you get sick, and the only way to fight the sickness is to use more." "So, the only time B.J is in a good mood is when he's high?" asked Gold. "You can say that," she nodded. He kept going, "Why do you continue to be with him?" "Because he must help me take care of this baby," she answered back in a depressed voice. You could hear in her voice that she couldn't believe she had waited almost sixteen years to have a baby by a heroin addict.

It was soon after the conversation with his mother that Gold made up his mind to work as hard as possible in school so he could get a scholarship and go off to college. But he also felt he had to do something to help B.J for the sake of his unborn sister. He knew he didn't have to deal with B.J's and his mother's lifestyle for much longer, but he refused to see his baby sister go though the same hell he was now experiencing.

When B.J came home the night Young Gold and his mother talked, she told him about Gold's feelings. He promised her he would get his life together and leave the drugs alone. He laid in bed for three days trying to kick his heroin habit and almost died. When Gold saw B.J's reaction from not using heroin, he realized how serious the drug was. B.J sweated, vomited, coughed, tossed and turned the whole time he was in bed, but he could not kick his habit. In the three days he was sick, B.J got motivated to start living again. He realized that there was more to life than getting high. He finally recognized that his money was short, and that within a few weeks his daughter was going to be born, so he planned to make another trip to Chicago. He had close to five thousand dollars. He was only short about another thousand from buying two ounces of heroin. The turnover from six thousand dollars could easily bring in sixteen thousand. It didn't make sense to go to Chicago and only buy one ounce, so he kept buying little packages in the city trying to make the other thousand he needed. But neither the quantity nor the quality was enough to both support his habit and make the money he needed.

Gold still had a lot of money saved. He thought loaning B.J money to get his package might be the thing to do to help his baby sister who would arrive any day. It was still hard for Young Gold to believe that a hundred thousand dollars had dwindled to four thousand in less than a year. He used to think about what big college he would attend, the cars he would buy, and all the designer clothes he would wear if all that money were his. And now it was gone. Gold had faith that B.J could fill up the safe once again, and loaned him the thousand dollars he needed for his package and five hundred more for traveling. B.J was very thankful, and Sparkle wanted to cut Gold's throat because she knew B.J's habit was too bad for him to get back on his feet without professional help.

B.J made two successful trips to Chicago and bought his newborn baby girl, Tara, all the clothes and items she might need during the next two years before he got caught on the highway. One weekend, he and Mark were on their way back with four ounces of heroin when they were pulled over by the police. More than a gram of heroin in some states carries a sentence of life in prison, so they were lucky when the cops simply took the drugs and sent them on their way. B.J and Mark thought they were doing the smart thing by driving, but in the drug business there is no smart way to do anything. First, they had sixteen thousand dollars taken by the police at the airport. Then they had their drugs taken by the same people who they purchased them from. It turned out that the two police officers that pulled B.J and Mark over on the highway were not real police officers. They worked for the guys who sold the drugs to them. Young Gold never got his money back from B.J, and Sparkle ended up raising Tara alone because after the first two years, B.J let his habit take him back to jail for committing petty crimes just to get a fix.

Chapter 12

It was a good thing Gold's grandfather, L.C started coming around showing interest in him during those high school years. If he had not been there to support Young Gold, the only male influence he would have had would have been B.J's. But Gold's grandfather rarely missed Gold's basketball games and track meets. Even on early Saturday mornings when Gold was involved in something, his grandfather would come straight from his third shift job at the bank to see him compete. He may have taken a little nap during the time he was there, but he was always present at events to support Gold. Gold's grandfather saw how much he loved school and pushed Gold to do his best at all times. L.C advised, "You never know who is watching you; your athletics along with your academics may help you get a scholarship to college, boy." Even before Gold's grandfather came fully into his life, Gold had tried to model his life after him and his Uncle Ward. He always heard his mother praising them: "My youngest brother Ward played football in college, and my dad played a few years of semi-pro ball." It was from hearing about their accomplishments that Gold gained encouragement. Knowing that athletics on a college or professional level were in his blood made him eager to succeed. With B.J in his life and the OLE Man not around, Gold needed positive encouragement and guidance because B.J and his mother made life a living hell during his first two and a half years of high school. When B.J finally moved out of the way, Sparkle again pulled herself together. She was doing all she could to send Gold to college and to raise her two and a half-year-old toddler.

Gold had often dreamed of going to the University of Michigan. His grandmother, April, had gone to Michigan State, but as a child he had liked the blue and gold better than the green and white. He saw their success in and fell in love with the Wolverines. His grandfather wanted him to go to Miami of Ohio because that was where his Uncle Ward graduated. But Gold was turned off because Miami was so far away. Gold and his mother wracked their brains the entire last half of his senior year trying to decide on a school. He had a Nike shoe box full of letters from colleges all over the country. Every day he went through his shoebox rereading his letters and brochures along with the new ones that arrived daily. Sparkle really didn't care what college Young Gold chose. She was just glad and proud he was headed in the right direction after all she had taken him through. But a secret he was holding inside did not make him feel proud of himself.

Chapter 13

By the end of the final grading period, Young Gold had narrowed his possibilities down to Michigan, Eastern Michigan, Cincinnati, and a private University near Toledo. His ambition told him to follow his dreams and go on to Michigan, but his heart told him to choose the school closest to home. He was a little afraid of leaving his mother because he knew she needed him to keep her in line and out of the streets. But his secret was the biggest reason he was having so much trouble choosing a school. He knew his mother's high educational expectations, and instead of telling her what was troubling him, he ignored it until graduation.

May 22, 1993 Commencement had arrived for Gold. He did not know whether to be happier than ever or to dig himself a hole in case his secret was discovered. Gold had everything to be proud of. He sat in the front seat of the front row on-stage, showing he was in the top twenty-five of his class. He was thanked by the Valedictorian for being a great class treasurer and leader. The principal wished him and the other track runners good luck at the state meet the following day. All of his family members were there to congratulate and praise him for going on to college that Fall. He seemed to be a king sitting on a throne.

When the graduation ceremony ended everybody gathered in the hall where all of Gold's close friends and teachers congratulated him and wished him good luck. His mother and grandmother congratulated all of his friends that they knew and asked them about their future plans. Gold's ex-girlfriend, Ann, was in the same graduating class. They had gone out from the middle of their sophomore year until the middle of their senior year. Out of all Gold's close classmates, she was the only one he prayed his mother and grandmother wouldn't see. But they both loved Ann, so that was only going to happen if she left the face of the earth. "Oh, how are you doing, Baby; we haven't seen you in a while?" Sparkle and April both said to Ann. She replied, "I've been doing fine," and turned red as an apple. Gold listened to their conversation from a distance, trying not to be noticed. He knew it was all over for him. He didn't know which was going to make his mother angrier. The fact that he had gotten Ann pregnant or that she was going to have a biracial grandchild. He could easily see Ann's six-month-old pregnant stomach sticking out of her red gown from where he was standing, so he knew his mother and grandmother noticed she was pregnant.

When Young Gold and his family left the restaurant that evening, his mother pulled him aside and asked, "Why didn't you tell me Ann was pregnant?" "I don't know; it's not mine," he answered. "Well, if it is your baby, you are going to take care of it because I raised you better than that," she announced as they walked out the door. He knew in his heart the baby was his all along, but he was afraid if he claimed the baby his mother would not let him go off to college. There was nothing in the world he wanted more than his education. He prayed every night, right up until the day he went off to college that everything would turn out so that he could continue his education, and be a father to his child. Sparkle bought him a cell phone so she could call and inform him of Ann's progress. He came home from school two weekends in a row to be with Ann for the birth of their baby, but their son wasn't ready to come.

On the night of September 2, 1993, Young Gold returned earlier than usual to the dormitory after dinner. He had a funny feeling there was an important message on his voice-mail. When he checked, there were two messages, but both were hang-ups. So he decided to call home and check on things. Sparkle answered the phone, impatient, "Hold on, Baby. No, I'll call you right back. Ann's on the other line in labor at the hospital." Gold's Aunt China was the first one at the hospital. She was going to be first to welcome her first great nephew into the world. Gold's whole family was enthusiastic about the birth of the family's next male to lead a generation. Gold's Great-grandmother Anita was the most excited. She had long waited to see her family again form five living generations. Gold could not believe he was in his freshman year of college and about to become a father. He was a nervous wreck all night, pacing back and forth across the floor of his dorm room, as if he was in the waiting room of the hospital.

Around 9:30 p.m. the phone had rang. Gold was across the hall talking to some friends, but before the phone could ring a second time he had flown back into his room, almost knocking down his Korean roommate to answer the phone. It was his mother. "She had him; she had him; we'll call you back from the hospital!" she shouted with great excitement. Gold settled down a little, but he was still unsure about how he was going to take care of his son while he was two hours from home.

Forty-five minutes later, Gold finally got a phone call from the hospital. It was mostly his family and Ann's friends who were present. Her family wanted nothing to do with her or her biracial son, Roland J. Gold. But after his first year into the world, no one could resist him. Sparkle had promised Gold that she would help him maintain his basic fatherly responsibilities as long as he did well in school, but every weekend that he did not have a track or cross-country meet, he would have to come home to be with his son. Roland J. also helped her keep her own life together. She did not want him to witness any of the things Gold had witnessed as a child. She now had two men of her own to keep her strong. Plus the OLE Man started coming back around to help her because he knew Gold had gone off to school.

Everything was working out fine for Gold. All of the stress from his son was off him, and he began a successful freshman year at a private University near Toledo. He stood out as a freshman in all of his cross-country meets that fall. He placed in the top 35 in the All-Ohio meet with over three hundred competing runners. And he did not miss a beat in the classroom. His grade card for the first semester had "B's" all the way down. Then, three weeks into the second semester, Sparkle took her second step backwards, and things got crazy when she let Silver back in her life.

Chapter 14

Sparkle accepted Silver back into her life only as a friend and a way of making quick money like in the past. She made it well understood that this was the way the relationship had to be. Silver couldn't accept the rejection, and the fact that things wouldn't be the same between them. When Silver was released from jail for stabbing the white man, he took a step that not only stabbed her in the back but upset the harmony of the family's life -- he started a relationship with her sister Rachel. Rachel had already given the family problem after problem by neglecting her two children and running wild, using drugs, and now the lowest thing she did was to take up a life with Silver. They moved back into the house he had shared with Tia. He started out on the right track, working for a construction company, but within a year he went right back to the drugs. He had formed the attitude that he could handle any amount of any drug on the streets. Which was very sad, because he had Rachel thinking the same thing. Every day, all day, it was party time at Rachel and Silver's house. Everybody in the city knew about the wood stained house on Nix. Silver was the richest crack smoker in Dayton. He had never lost his ability to make money. Whatever it took for him to support his five hundred-dollar a day drug habit, he did. Stealing was his specialty. No store in America without a surveillance camera stood a chance of catching him. He made sure he was going to get high, and that everyone in the house was going to eat. He would go to the grocery store with five dollars and come back with enough food to feed ten adults. He would stuff steaks all the way around his waist and then go to the counter and pay for a loaf of bread, canned goods, and a box of mashed potatoes. His heart was braver than a lion's. He would break into people's garages in broad daylight and take their lawn mowers, weed eaters, and gas cans. Then he would be bold enough to go a couple blocks away and cut grass, house to house, for money. By the end of the day he would have made over two hundred dollars, but it all went to the drug dealers along with the lawn mower, weed eater, and the gas can when the money ran out.

About a year after Silver and Rachel were together she got pregnant. All the women in Gold's family were fertile. Rachel already had two children, but it had never dawned on her and Silver to use protection during sex since they both were heavily using drugs. With the lifestyle they were living, sexual transmitted diseases were not on their minds, but bringing a helpless, suffering crack baby into the world should have been. All through Rachel's pregnancy, she and Silver continued to get high the same as they did before she got pregnant. The night she went into labor she was so high she didn't even realize she was about to give birth. K.C had to stay in the hospital for nearly a month after his birth. His little lungs and bloodstream were so full of chemicals from drugs that the doctors didn't expect him to live. Children's Services Bureau did a mini investigation, but quickly closed the case. Silver and Rachel were so strung out on drugs that when K.C was allowed to leave the hospital neither of them bothered to show up. This was one of the hospital's first situations like it. They were going to send K.C to Children's Services, when his great-grandmother Anita rescued him.

Silver let himself go to hell again. The year after K.C was born he lost his house, his hustle, and his manhood. He had nowhere to go. His drug habit was so bad that none of his family members trusted him to stay in their home, fearing he would bring trouble by stealing to buy drugs. Silver went from a sophisticated classy man to a homeless bum living on the streets, sleeping under bridges, using cardboard boxes to stay warm, while Rachel took her two oldest children from family member to family member while she ran the streets.

It made Anita's blood boil to know Rachel and Silver had no intentions of taking care of K.C. And now that they had no place to live, she was stuck with him. She realized if she gave K.C back to Rachel, he would be dropped off on someone else just like her other two children. So she went through all the legal procedures to maintain full custody. It was a huge responsibility for a sixty-seven year old woman, but she found a soft place in her heart and let Rachel and Silver move into the other side of her duplex, hoping they would lend a hand, and get their lives together.

Rachel settled down a lot because she respected her grandmother. She still got high a little bit, but it was much milder than when she and Silver lived on Nix. She got away from heavy drugs. She would smoke a marijuana joint and sniff a few lines when she could afford it, but since Silver was not around as much, neither was crack. He didn't last living next door to Anita because his drug habit gave him a very disrespectful attitude. He did not care anymore. In a sane world, it would seem that Silver would have changed for his children. But even after he and Rachel had two more children, his attitude did not improve, it worsened. He would rob the neighborhood drug dealers and run back to Anita's house -- jeopardizing his life, Rachel's life, her grandmother's life, and his children's lives. The only thing on Silver's mind was how he was going to get another piece of crack. He even got sloppy with his stealing. Instead of checking to see if anyone in the store was watching him, he would just go in and start stuffing items. And it was on one of the afternoons when he was desperately stealing for his first high of the day that he was caught. When he went to court, the judge was going to drop the theft charges and send him to a drug rehabilitation center, but Silver told him to kiss his black ass and attempted to spit on him. The police officers in the courtroom quickly wrestled him down and carried him off. Silver was having withdrawal symptoms that day in court from not having any crack in his system for two days. He wasn't able to control himself. But the three years in prison he brought on himself did some good.

The next time Silver got out of jail he came to reality. He realized his children were important, and that they needed him in their lives. During the three years in jail he gained back some of his dignity, manhood, and his pride. It was to bad that Rachel was living in Crestmore, acting like a teenager, so Silver had to get right down to business. He appreciated Sparkle helping her get an apartment after their grandmother put her and the children out. Even though he and Rachel had gone behind her back, Sparkle could not see her nieces and nephews in the street. Anita did not care. She was fed up with Rachel. She couldn't deal any longer with Rachel's wild lifestyle next door to her. She had helped Rachel as much as she could. She was taking care of K.C and Rachel's oldest child, letting Rachel live there for free, and feeding the other three children. Anita was getting too old. She wanted to live in peace, and it was just impossible with Rachel there.

When Silver came home it was not easy for him to come right into his children's lives and gain their respect. They knew Silver was their father, but he had never spent time with them. In the beginning, they paid him as much attention as they paid Rachel. It was near the end of

October, so giving the children their first real Christmas would help. With the little money he came home with, he bought them a pair of shoes and put clothes on their backs. Rachel did not care if they had clothes or not. As long as she had money for a blunt and a beer, life was peachy cream.

Silver's little money did not last long. The odd jobs he worked were not going to allow him to make enough money to give his children the type of Christmas he had planned, so he had to come up with something. It took him no time to see that he was in the middle of the promise land for drug activity, and the queen of it all was the woman he had always loved. In the back of his mind he knew Sparkle could help him get back on his feet because she knew everybody. But at the time, she was involved with a guy name Jerry. He was a good honest workingman who knew nothing of the streets. He was by far the best man Sparkle had in her life since Gold's father. He did not get high, respected her to the highest degree, and did everything he could to help her and Gold. She ruined the best thing she ever had going -- for Silver.

Chapter 15

Gold was glad to see Silver trying to get his life together, but he wished it were with another woman. Gold felt his mother should have lost every feeling she ever had for Silver when he had left them to die over the stolen drugs, and more so, when he had three children with Rachel. Gold could not believe his mother let Silver back into her life. But nothing amazed him with the women in his family when it came to men. One weekend Gold came home from school and Silver was staying at Rachel's house. Then, two weekends later he was living with Sparkle. It was true that Silver acted like a totally different person when he was with Sparkle. He went to work, helped out with the bills, and provided for his children, but without trust, there's nothing.

Sparkle allowed Silver to nearly destroy the strong young man she had created. Gold was highly influenced by Silver because he was the first man Gold had taken liking to. When Gold and his college friends came home on weekends, Silver told them stories about how he use to run the streets making money, gambling, and chasing women. There was no reason to question him because ever since he got back with Sparkle he had been making money. Most of Gold's friends were upper class men, but the things about the streets that Silver told were new to them. At eighteen Gold already had more than enough knowledge about the streets. Not wanting to get involved with the lifestyle of the streets, and adopt the gangster mentality had been the main force pushing him towards college. He hated jail from visiting his uncle Eric as a kid, and he had escaped death many times through the drama with his mother, so Gold knew the streets was not the life he wanted to live.

When school let out that summer, Gold got his same summer job back working for the county. He had worked there the previous two summers, but this year he had intentions to save enough money to get an apartment of his own. When Roland J. was born, he and his mother agreed that at the end of the school year he would transfer to Dayton University because it was closer to home. All of Gold's peers who lived in Crestmore were still there, doing the same old thing. When he first went to college, the dropouts and the older guys were hanging out, smoking marijuana and selling drugs. It surprised him to see some of the guys he had went to school with and even graduated with joining them. The same group of people Gold had tried to avoid when he first moved to Crestmore was now running the complex. Crestmore was a one-stop-shop-drug-spot. You could find crack, cocaine, marijuana, pills, heroin, and any other illegal drug on the market there.

The OLE Man helped Sparkle and Gold the whole time Gold was at school. Some weekends, when Gold did not have a ride home, the OLE Man drove up to school and got him. He understood how important it was for a father to be in his child's life. He did not mind doing what he could to bring Gold and Roland J. together. That summer the OLE Man knew Gold was trying to get established so he could continue school and take care of Roland J. Over the summer, instead of driving himself on his business trips, he paid Gold two hundred dollars a month to drive for him. His eyes couldn't handle the eight-hour road trips like they use to. He'd much rather pay Young Gold out of his pocket for driving than see him get money in the streets as Silver showed him. It was bad enough that Gold sold marijuana to friends from school, and to a few people in Crestmore that he trusted. The OLE man did not want to see Gold get into the life of a hustler because he had so much going for himself. The OLE Man had been there, and he knew Gold was not cut out for that life. Gold was too strong and too focused to let any of the guys in Crestmore persuade him to sell drugs and cause him to miss out on his promising future. But when Silver sold two ounces of cocaine to two undercover cops in a suburban town and asked Gold to get rid of the drugs left behind to get him a lawyer, the OLE Man panicked. He knew Gold's nineteen-year-old mind didn't really comprehend what Silver was asking him to do. In so many words, Silver was asking Gold to risk his life to help save his own. Gold thought about it for a few days. He tried to talk it over with his mother, but Silver had turned her back onto the drugs, and she was no help.

Gold was born into a family of hustlers, so what Silver was asking was nothing new to him. The streets were where every man Young Gold knew got their money. But Young Gold also knew where the life of a drug dealer could lead if you were not careful. Plus, he had learned a lot from the drug trafficking case Silver had just caught. On his way to a lawyer to deliver the money and Silver's discovery packet, Gold read the paperwork to see how the narcotics police unit had set Silver up. Gold had heard of the term discovery packet, but he hadn't known what it was. It contained all the evidence of a crime the prosecutor intended to use against the accused in court. There were photocopies of every dollar bill given to Silver in exchange for the drugs, pictures of him during the transactions, and a list of times, dates, and quantities of narcotics that had been purchased.

The police narcotics unit had caught on to Silver's operation when the deputy sheriffs went into Rachel's apartment. They had seized over six thousand dollars worth of furniture and Christmas gifts that Silver had gotten in a trade for drugs to a crack-head who had cleared out his wife's and kid's house a week before Christmas. The deputies already had the crack-head in custody, so there was no receiving-stolen-property charge filed. They couldn't charge Silver because it was Rachel's house, but they did start watching him. He had always been money hungry, and did not care what he had to do for a dollar. In the streets, as long as a person had money, Silver provided the product.

The narcotics police unit sent a light skinned business-like police informant to buy crack for almost seven months straight from Silver. The informant wouldn't spend less than a hundred dollars, and he would only deal with Silver. The other dealers in Crestmore tried their hardest to sell to him, but he stayed loyal to Silver. One day he asked, "Can you get a hold of some big pieces for my friends out in Central Valley?" Silver did not hesitate because he knew with them being from the suburbs he could jack the price up. But in the beginning, he would take one of his workers with him, and give them a piece of the money for making the transaction. After Silver got comfortable with the two white guys, he made the transactions himself.

On the night they arrested Silver, the police informant called him to say that his guys wanted to buy two ounces of cocaine at 9 o'clock that night. The two undercover cops Silver was to meet watched Sparkle's apartment all that day waiting for the perfect time to arrest him. Silver was out most of the day making runs, and when he came home that night, shortly after sunset, the two undercover cops and a deputy sheriff met him at Sparkle's doorstep. Silver ran upstairs to the bathroom and sat on the toilet real quick to get rid of the drugs he had on him. He intended to escape, but there was only one way in and one way out Sparkle's apartment, so he was trapped.

Silver faced eight to ten years. The attorney he selected to take his case asked for five thousand dollars up front, and three thousand dollars by the day of the trial. Silver felt he had a chance to beat the case because the photographs did not reveal the person's entire face, just a rear and side view. It only took Gold three days to come up with the first five thousand dollars, and the next morning Mr. Chomsky visited Silver in jail to discuss the case. After a month of reviewing and making deals with the prosecutor, Mr. Chomsky could only guarantee Silver three years off his sentence. Silver knew he would have gotten five years with a court appointed attorney, so he had wasted five thousand dollars. Silver cussed out Mr. Chomsky so badly that he dropped the case without refunding Silver one dollar. He did not have the other three thousand dollars he needed for Mr. Chomsky, anyway, because Young Gold had come to his senses and began hustling for himself. In addition to Silver's money, he had already put in an additional fifteen hundred dollars. Gold woke up one day and decided, "If I am going to risk my life in these streets, I'm going to hustle for myself."

While the dealers in Crestmore were running up to cars selling ten and twenty dollar pieces, Gold was in big cities hooking up with guys who paid him five thousand dollars or more just to make deliveries. God had blessed Gold with the gift of seeing life through other people's eyes. All the men Sparkle had brought into Gold's life were hustlers. He saw that when the men in his mother's life took their business out of town where they were less known that the streets were more prosperous for them. Gold saw that any hustler could make money in their hometown, but the more they got the more eyes they opened. On the down side, Gold saw many of his mother's friends, and family members fall to the street from greed and using to much of the drug that they sold, or from drug use period. By reflecting on the situations that he had been through as a child, he knew how to get on top. Gold knew he had a prosperous life ahead of him and took the street life as a game. But by the time he turned twenty-one, he did not want to play anymore.

Chapter 16

To Gold, the streets had become a giant hole, like ones in the jungle used to capture wild animals. He found out that in the streets you have no friends and that there is no one you can trust. Within one week he lost fifteen thousand dollars to one of the nickel and dime drug dealers in Crestmore and another twenty-five thousand dollars to the mother of his second son. He had trusted Pam with everything, but wasn't ready to settle down. When rumors reached her that he was involved with someone else, she ran off with his child and his money. She never returned despite her actions putting her and her family's lives in danger. On the other hand, Gold had many chances to kill the dealer who broke into Sparkle's apartment and stole the fifteen thousand. Even though Skull fled to another state, Gold received phone calls from people in the city and business partners from five other states offering to hunt Skull down and kill him. But Gold had to be careful because Pam had gone to the police for protection. She told everything she knew about Gold: the different cars he drove, his residences within the city and out of town, how he made his money, and the names of everybody on his team that she knew. Everyone in the city knew about the stolen money, and if Skull would had been found dead right away, all fingers would have pointed at Gold. Gold also thought about his son, Roland J. The whole purpose of Gold moving closer to home was to take care of him. Which would be impossible to do from a prison cell or while on the run. Both Pam and Skull thought they had hurt Gold and put him on his back. But after a month's vacation with some of his rich buddies in Atlanta, Gold cleared his mind of the lost forty thousand dollars and used it as a wake-up call. The game was over for him. Gold was about to turn twenty-two, and was looking for a way out of the streets. He set a two hundred and fifty dollar a day savings goal, and prayed that by the time he was twenty-five his life would be back on track. Every night before he laid down his head, he thanked God for helping him make progress that day, and asked him to continue helping him climb out of the streets. The dealers in Crestmore and other people in the streets did not believe Young Gold was human. He shook off a forty thousand dollar loss like it was a mere forty dollars, and two months later he was again living like a king. He cut off association with everybody. He took care of all his business by himself or with the OLE Man. He was on a mission to make as much money as he could in one year so he could go back to college and show the two people who had betrayed his trust that there was a lot more money where the other had come from.

It took Sparkle almost a year to even realize how deeply Young Gold was involved in the streets. He had given up on school because of the street habits he adopted, and he was in too deeply for her to change his mind about things. Gold had started drinking, gambling, and hustling just like everyone else who hung in Crestmore. After class, instead of going to the library to complete a required assignment or to do required research, Gold would come back to Crestmore and see how much money he could make. All the guys who didn't like him when they were younger, really hated him when school was out that summer. He took over the whole apartment complex without even knowing. It amazed them that a college square jumped in the street game, and made more money in two years than they had in ten. Gold was making so much money hustling that a huge green cloud shrouded his education.

The women in Gold's family felt guilt when they saw what the streets did to him. His grandmother, his mother, and his Aunt Rachel were discussed with everyone pointing fingers and blaming each other for Gold's involvement in the streets. They had never expected their golden child to become a hustler. He had fought it all his life, but when Sparkle brought Silver back into her life, the life that Gold had been eagerly trying to avoid ever since he was six years old sprouted. And then everything went wrong. Instead of advising him to stay in school, they thrived on his gambling and hustling because they could have extra money for whatever they wanted. They did not see anything wrong with Gold's hustling once they saw him prospering. Their attitude came from years of attachment to men living that lifestyle. They thought it was normal, and Young Gold felt it was in his genes to hustle. Because that was the life that they were all comfortable with, there was no one in Gold's family to pull him aside, to let him know that the streets were full of misery and back-stabbing. It took the only mature man who had ever entered Gold's family to save him.

Chapter 17

The OLE Man expressed his discomfort with Gold's gambling and hustling to April because he did not feel it was his place to directly approach Gold. "You better talk to that boy before he messes up his life; he's being too careless with them streets," he told her. She insisted, "You're the only man he has in his life; you need to talk to him." "You know how these kids act today, they don't listen to no damn body," he responded. "He's not like that, he'll listen, he'll listen," April argued. The OLE Man was truly Gold's guardian angel. That whole year Gold prayed for a way out of the streets, and the OLE Man stayed with him each step of the way. He did not want to be authoritative. He just wanted Gold to accomplish the educational dreams and goals he had planned, and leave the streets to someone who had a lot more knowledge of them.

It came to a point when Young Gold did not have to worry about paying the bills, providing food for his family, or worry about where money was going to come from for him to get back and forth to school because the OLE Man always came though. Gold now had free time to concentrate on what was important in life to him. The OLE Man put a silver spoon in Gold's mouth just as the women in his family did when he was born. Everything was handed to him. Gold started to enjoy life as he had done when he was in school, and when his family had been pushing him. The OLE Man opened Gold's eyes so he could see that his education and his family were both still there waiting for him; all he had to do was go and get them.

In the Winter Quarter of 1997 Young Gold enrolled part-time at the University of Cincinnati, and started remodeling the ancestral home his great-great-grandmother Rosey had left behind when he was twelve. He decided it was finally time to show his family he was ready to be the chief of their clan. Sparkle had named him after a general of The Black Liberation Army, so it was meant for him to be a leader. While Gold was remodeling the family house, he was also remodeling the family. He tried to start with the generations before his, but he quickly realized they were fixed in their ways, so he turned his focus to his own generation. He was majoring in Elementary Education, so the other twenty children of his generation were a good start. He hoped when the older family members recognized how he was starting a trend that would ensure his generation did not come up as they had done, perhaps they all would follow. But things did not quite work out like Gold expected. He had his generation on the right track, but the women in the older generation continued to be plagued with negative men from outside the family. All of Gold's dreams and goals were near fulfillment when Silver came back to interfere for a third time.

While Silver was in prison, Young Gold sent him money every month or when he called and was in need. Silver heard from other prisoners who came in during his sentence how well Gold was doing in the streets. "Young Gold is running Crestmore; he gets all the money," they would say. When Silver came home he felt Gold owed him because it was his money that had started Gold's street success. He could not comprehend how Young Gold jumped in the game for three years, and jumped back out with what it had taken him twenty-five years and three trips to prison to get. Silver thought he was going to come home and run Gold's family like he did in the past, but Gold was a made man now. Everyone looked up to him because he had stopped hustling and was doing something positive with his life. And with the OLE Man by his side, Silver did not stand a chance of messing things up even when Sparkle let him back into her life. The OLE Man was there every day to make sure Silver took care of business. Silver went to work for the city's largest construction company, and to the family house to give Gold a hand remodeling. It made Silver proud to see all the positive things Gold was doing because he saw a lot of himself in Young Gold, yet his manhood could not bare the jealously.

Silver was used to being in control, moving freely, and doing what he wanted to do. But now that Young Gold was older, he and the OLE Man made sure that as long as Silver was with Sparkle he respected the family. In January of 1999 the OLE Man passed away. Silver did not give him six months in his grave before he tried to take over. Everyone thought that when the OLE Man passed, Sparkle would get her life together, but she quickly got worse because of Silver. She was on drugs stronger than ever. The two of them would stay up all night, getting high, and sleep all day like vampires. She never left the house and he left only to get more drugs or to get food for the children. She constantly cleaned the house because the cocaine in her system made her body speed, unable to sit down and relax. Silver had Sparkle so drugged out, she was allowing him to spend time with Rachel all day, and come home to her at night.

"The OLE Man got to be turning in his grave," thought Gold. He knew the OLE Man's sprit was with him, ensuring he continued his education and carried the family, but Gold was going crazy trying to get his mother to put Silver out of her life for good. Gold was having enough trouble trying to get over the OLE Man's sudden death, and the situation with his mother and Silver made Gold want to join him. The OLE Man's death reinforced Gold's understanding that there were no men in the family beside him, and it was up to him to change things. The OLE Man had been a part of Gold's life for twelve years and had made such an impact on the family that Gold had forgotten the OLE Man was not related by blood. When Sparkle was a young girl, the OLE Man had lived next door to the family up on Sugar Hill, but Gold hadn't been introduced to him until his Grandma April brought him into the family. The relationship the OLE Man, Sparkle, and Gold shared was unusual for people of no kin. From sunup to sundown, the OLE Man and Sparkle knew where the other was, what each other was doing, and who each was doing it with. If his wife or anyone in his family wanted to know where the OLE Man was, they called Sparkle. During the two years the OLE Man was helping Gold get his life together, it had became a habit for him to visit the OLE Man every day after class. And when he passed away, Gold was stuck looking for another man in the family to take his place, and there was no one. His Grandma April was the only one available for him to turn to, and she was not much help at first because she had lost her faith.

Chapter 18

April was sixty years old, living in remission from cancer, and driving herself crazy over her eighty year old drug dependent mother, her incarcerated son, her two drug dependent daughters who were in love with the same man, and the well being of her twenty-two grandchildren and six great-grandchildren. She was pulled in a hundred different directions, but was also the only one sane enough to get Young Gold through his tragic loss of the OLE Man. The night of the funeral, Gold let his tears pour on his grandma's shoulder because it was killing him to realize there was no man in the family he could turn to. He felt just as lost and betrayed, as did the women in his family. But Young Gold also knew the OLE Man's death was his cue to take over, and his grandma convinced him that the OLE Man would always be with him in spirit.

Young Gold was exhausted with the thought there was no male figure in his family beside himself. It hurt, but it started making sense to him why his mother dealt with the low caliber of men that she did. Gold felt the only way that he could strongly attempt to change things for his generation, and truly save his mother from the hands of men like Silver, was to find out more about his ancestry, especially the males. He wanted to know about the men whom he came from because they had so completely failed to be a major part of his life and his mother's life. Young Gold hoped by learning more about the men in his great-great grandma Rosey's life, his great-grandma Anita's life, and his grandma April's life that he would better understand why his mother was so attracted to street men. But he also wanted to know where he came from to better understand who he was, and why he had lived such a rough life in his twenty-four years. He thought it would be nice to know that one of his ancestors had been an important person. Someone during their lifetime that may had been a king or queen of some Aztec or African tribe, a famous inventor of something we use every day, or a great leader of the civil rights movement.

Gold started to study and read about the science of genealogy so he could learn about his roots. He found that his mother's behavior had been passed to her from previous generations. Young Gold used the book "How To Find Your Family Roots" by William Latham as a guide because the author illustrated simple options in conducting an ancestral search. The most basic way to begin the search was to first examine yourself, and then go back as far as you could on both your mother's and father's sides of the family, gathering as much accurate information that was available. Gold was only interested in his mother's side of the family, so he used Latham's suggestion to interview the older members of the family.

The OLE Man's funeral was held in the middle of January, so Young Gold only had about eight months until his twenty-fifth birthday. This meant he only had eight months left to achieve the dreams and goals he had set two years ago when the OLE Man helped him leave the streets. Young Gold was the oldest member of the fourth generation out of the five living, so the information he sought came easily. He had the opportunity to enjoy his great-great grandma Rosey's company first-hand for twelve years. There was no man in Rosey's life because her husband had passed before Young Gold was born. He had never heard her talk about his great-great grandpa Kilmery C. Brent, but he had seen pictures of her husband Henry James Sr.

Rosey was a disciplinarian and a very strict religious woman. She celebrated her Sabbath on Saturday's because she was a Seventh Day Adventist. Young Gold had no choice but to spend his early Saturday mornings attending church services with her because she was strict about attending church. He would whine often about missing Saturday morning cartoons, but once he was there bible study was enjoyable to him. Plus, when church service ended, he knew Rosey would fill his pockets with peppermints. She always kept a bag of peppermints in her black purse and in the bottom drawer of her refrigerator. In Gold's lifetime the only Saturdays she missed church were when she was in the hospital near death, a time very vague to him even though he had been twelve at the time. He had loved her and spent as much time with her as he had with the OLE Man, but he had not felt the same pain when he lost her. Nothing Gold remembered about Rosey reflected the lifestyle of his mother, so he took his investigation deeper and found that his sweet great-great-grandma Rosey had not always been so sweet. In her younger days, she would rant and rave up and down the street, cussing out the white venders who came into her neighborhood to sell their produce. And on weekends she would go to the bootleg joint down the street from her house and get dripping wet drunk. Poor Henry would come home from his hard labor job and catch hell on Friday nights. He had fought in World War I, but he curled up in his rocking chair and read his newspaper when Rosey was full of juice. Now Gold knew from where his mother, his aunts, his grandma April, and his great-grandma Anita got their loud mouths, and their evil streak. On many occasions they hurt people's feelings because they did not bite their tongues.

Anita, Gold's great-grandmother, was the oldest living member of the family. He went to her first for information, but to Young Gold she only revealed the positive things about everyone's life because she did not want him to know she had started the heartache and pain he had gone through so far in life. She told him how rich her husbands were, and how well they provided for her and her children, but she never once mentioned her first husband -- Gold's great-grandpa Flip Cole. Gold had asked her, "If everything was so perfect back then, why is our family so messed up now?" She could not explain what had happened, but went on to tell how she had bought her children and her grandchildren the best of everything, and how wealthy they had all lived. Young Gold knew there was a lot more to what his great-grandma Anita was telling, so he dug her past up himself.

Young Gold's great-grandma Anita was a very light complexioned pretty child. She was the oldest of Rosey's children, and one whose biological father was a man other than Henry James. Anita's father Kilmery was the son of a White Irishman man whom Rosey had been involved with when she was thirteen living on the plantation before her family were free. Anita and her brother Kilmery Jr. were the pick of the litter because their other brothers and sisters were a darker complexion that favored their father Henry. Anita spent most of her childhood with a high class, rich aunt and uncle in Philadelphia instead of with her mother. She grew into a very sophisticated beautiful lady who married three times and drove hundreds of men crazy. Her first husband was Flip Cole, Gold's great-grandpa. They became sweethearts during high school, but Rosey did not think he was the one for her stardom bound daughter, so she sent Anita to Philadelphia to keep them apart. Flip graduated in the first graduating Class of Dunbar High School in 1937, and then went on to become the first black to play on Dayton's semi-pro football team.

Anita and Flip's classmates always voted them best couple, and after Flip's football career ended, he went to Philadelphia to take Anita's hand in marriage. In 1939, they give birth to Gold's grandma, April Cole. And two years later they were divorced, but waiting the arrival of their second child, Bruce Cole, Young Gold's great uncle. Both April and Bruce remained close to their parents until Bruce was three years old and April was five years old. Flip went on the road to pursue a career as a musician, and Anita left the children with her mother Rosey, and went back to Philadelphia to live with her Aunt Joe who was a musician and her uncle who was a deacon of the church. To April and Bruce, it seemed that their out-of-state relatives were trying to steer their mother towards a different life style than she had at home, and it left them often missing her. Anita would come home to visit the children around their birthdays, but they spent most of their childhood with their grandma Rosey, their aunts, and their cousins.

In 1949, Anita came home to stay, and she brought exciting news with her for April and Bruce. She told them, "While I was away, I got married to a wealthy businessman and we're taking you to live with us." H.T was an uneducated man who could not drive or even count his money, but had a knack for making it. He ran a nightclub down on 5th street that brought in an enormous crowd every night of the week. Every night, when he closed up, he walked home holding a brown paper bag full of money. The luxurious environment April and Bruce moved into was finer than any type of lifestyle they had ever imagined. They quickly became rich, snobbish, high-class kids who wanted for nothing. April loved to go to school because she liked to learn, but

Bruce did not make it to the seventh grade. At every school he attended he got kicked out for trying to sleep with the teacher, or for actually sleeping with her. He was out of control because he was so handsome and so rich. He was just a man before his time. Their stepfather, H.T, took a lot of interest in Bruce, but April was troublesome because she still hungered for the love and company of her musician father, who could only write and phone because he was constantly on the road performing. Even though Flip was not in her life, she refused to let another man take his place. By the time April and Bruce got familiar with their stepfather's extravagant lifestyle, Anita divorced him and removed the children from H.T's custody. April was about thirteen and glad to leave because she could not deal with her beautiful mother being physically abused. Bruce, on the other hand, refused to leave, and stayed with H.T because he had grown accustomed to their rich lifestyle. Then, about six months later he came with his clothes to live with April and his mother. Anita took her money from the divorce and bought her a three-bedroom house in a predominantly white upper-class neighborhood where she ran a bootleg joint in the basement, so Bruce quickly flocked.

After Anita's divorce from H.T she stayed single for about two years until she met a big time gambler who came to the bootleg joint she ran downstairs in her basement of her house that she had brought with money from the divorce. She had to maintain the rich lifestyle she was accustomed to living, so her bootleg gambling joint in the basement became her hustle. She brought in six or seven hundred dollars a night because only the city's biggest gamblers came to her place. As beautiful as she was she caught everyone's eye that came in her place, and a big time guy named Thorn got the shot. He was a pimp, a dealer, and a killer. He had children by the battiest hustling woman in the city, but her moneymaking ability could not match Anita's beauty. She was a prize that he took and sent all over the country to show off. Thorn was so infatuated with her beauty that he trusted Anita to participate in his line of business. He sent her on first-class planes to Chicago, Detroit, and New York, two or three times a month, to pick up heroin packages. She would get on the plane in her mink coats and pearls, and no one ever suspected she had two to five kilos of heroin in her bag. She would meet Thorn at a racetrack or at a special event in the city where he had to take care of business. He was not allowed to come back to the city with his product. He worked for a big time gang that paid off the police to protect him when he brought the money into the city, but the police would not allow them to bring in drugs.

On Anita's last trip for Thorn she almost lost her life twice. She had been picking up and delivering packages for over a year when on her way from Detroit she decided to dip into the package while still on the plane. That wasn't her first time using heroin, but when she met Thorn at the racetrack in Cincinnati he wanted her to test it for him before he made the drop, and shortly after, she was rushed to the hospital. They thought she had ptomaine poisoning from a chilidog she had eaten, but she had overdosed on heroin. When she came home from the hospital, Thorn beat her to the point where she left him. April overheard Thorn beating her mother, but she never knew what for. When Anita left Thorn she was fed up with street man so she went to work for a local medical center doing physical therapy and turned the bootleg joint over to April and Bruce.

Anita's relationship with Thorn had ruined the lives of her children. At thirteen Bruce already had acquired the love for women. And when he started hustling for Thorn, the love for money, and drugs followed quickly. By age fifteen Thorn had pulled Bruce all the way into the streets. Thorn was getting old and the heroin and alcohol were taking a toll on his body; he needed someone to keep his money flowing, and Bruce had been around and knew what the game was all about.

While Anita was working long hours at the medical center and Bruce was major pimping and heroin dealing, April was searching for love. Gold's grandma April was not looking for a rich man. She just wanted a man to show her the love and affection she needed. L.C Young Gold's grandfather was from a poor family that got by on the money they made in his uncle's little corner store. His mother died when he was very young, so his grandmother and his father took care of him. L.C did not have a lot going for him in the beginning. But when he became a football star at Dunbar High School and started putting together the battiest hot rods in the city, all the girls fell in love with him. Anita hated that April was in love with L.C, because she did not feel his family was wealthy enough. He had to sneak over to the white side of town to see April because blacks got chased and beat for being on the side of town where April lived. L.C was nicknamed 'Blue Jesus' because he was so dark, but he made it to see April on enough occasions because by his senior year in high school she was pregnant. Anita, April's mom tried to make her get an abortion, but April wanted more than anything in the world to have L.C's baby. L.C was headed to college to play football and didn't acknowledge April after she told him she was pregnant. L.C was April's first hug, first kiss, first everything, and he told her, "It ain't mine."

After a short three-week stay at Green University, L.C came back home to help take care of his baby girl, Sparkle, and he married April. Right after Gold's mother was born his Uncle Lenny and his Aunt Rachel came back to back. April was eighteen with three children to raise and L.C had to give up football for employment to support her and the kids. L.C wasn't making enough money to support his family, and April could not work because she had to stay home to care for the children. April was living at home with Anita when Sparkle was born, but after the birth of Lenny and Rachel she was force to move into a project apartment community on the west side of Dayton.

L.C had hung in there for about three and a half years but the pressure of being twenty years old with a wife and three kids was just to much for him. After they divorced, he did what he could for the children and went on to play semi-pro football while April continued seeking for the right man to love her. She fell into many short-lived relationships with pimps and hustlers who wanted to beat her because she would not leave her children and sell her body for them. There was no way she could live as a prostitute, not when her father and her brother were the two biggest pimps in town.

April stayed at home with her three children being supported by welfare and her mother for about a year and then fell in love with an entertainer with whom she gave birth to three more children -- Gold's Uncle Eric, Aunt Mica, and Aunt China. Her love was not as strong for their father as it was for Gold's grandfather L.C. But during the three years of her and Victor T. Sams break-up, get back together, baby making marriage, the outcome was still the same.

Victor T. Sams was singing in a group with three of his friends when he and April first met. Then after their second child Mica was born Victor and his group started to travel performing at nights clubs in Dayton, Cincinnati, Chicago, Detroit, Harlem, and other cities throughout the Mid-west and the East Coast. He would be out of town for days and on occasions for weeks. It felt to April like she still was without a man, and now had five children without their father. It seemed as if Victor came home only to make babies because on a visit home before he and April's final break up, she got pregnant with Gold's Aunt China. He and his group were just signed to a major recording deal that went on to produce a few hit albums which cause him to be away from home more than ever. April had given up on Victor and moved on even though she knew it was going to be hell raising six children on her own. She was now twenty-one years old with no job on welfare living in a poverty-stricken project home community with six children.

Gold's great-grandma Anita was real fed up with Dayton. She was tired of April, her grand children, and Bruce. The bootleg joint went down the tubes within six months after she handed it over to the children, so she sold the house and moved to Chicago where she married Mr. Willis. His lifestyle was much slower than her first two husbands were. He was an older square man who owned a dry cleaners and gambled cards on the weekend. She had finally found a decent man who also had the wealth she always wanted. Even though she was now happily married and a way from the madness she worried about the well being of April, Bruce, and the children. Her big heart just could not let them go. She came back to Dayton and brought a huge stone six-bedroom house up on the hill, Sugar Hill. And with April still unemployed struggling with the children, Anita moved them out of the projects into the house with her. Bruce had quickly became rich working for Thorn, but by the time he was twenty-five he started to like what he was selling more than he liked to sell it. In some ways things for the family were looking up, but life in the fast lane was catching up.

Anita being back in town gave April a chance to get out and better herself. Mica, China, and Eric's father Victor T. Sams had finally settled down. The children visited him often for about two years then he was murdered. There were many rumors about why he was killed, but no one knew for sure because the murder was left unsolved. Sparkle was now in high school, Lenny and Rachel were on the verge of dropping out of the seventh and eight grade, Mica and Eric were in grade school, and China was still a baby. Anita thought she was helping out by moving back home, but the move on Sugar Hill brought everything downhill because of her involvement with Thorn again.

Bruce's business relationship with Thorn is what sparked things back up between Thorn and Anita. Bruce had a drug habit so bad now, that it did not allow him to make money anymore. He stayed in trouble with the law, and every heroin dealer in the city wanted to kill him. He had messed up so many of Thorn's heroin packages that Anita had to take out a loan on the house for Thorn to get back on his feet. Anita stuck around for a short while then went back to her husband in Chicago when old habits were becoming a problem for her.

April and the children continued to live in the house on Sugar Hill, but it was not as enjoyable as it was in the beginning with the police visiting every other day looking for Bruce. He would usually hide leaving one of the teenagers at the door to lie, and say he wasn't there. April was teaching head start school during the hours the police usually visited, so she was in the dark on what was going on. She was in her own world anyway. She was working outside of the house away from her children, and had finally been rescued by a wealthy loving man who excepted her and all six of her children.

Up until Gold's mother Sparkle was in her junior year in high school they lived up on the hill. April's new love Mr. Charles had started paying the mortgage bill from the loan that Anita took out for Thorn, then stopped when he decided to make April his wife. In the beginning he just did not want to see April and the kids in the street. He had many pieces of his own property that were paid for. He felt Thorn was not making any attempt to pay on the loan so why should he.

One afternoon a teacher that April worked with informed her that she saw police and mover trucks in April's front yard coming back from her lunch break. When April arrived home everything she owned was stacked on the side of the road. Police cars and mover trucks were parked on the hill of the front lawn, and the big mansion style home was no more. The family had lost the house on Sugar Hill because the package that was brought with the loan money only profited a great high for Thorn and Bruce. Anita was still in Chicago with no knowledge that she had lost her home, and April and the children had to move in with Mr. Charles.

When Anita came home and found out that April and Mr. Charles had stopped paying on the loan she was distraught. That was all that she had left to show for all of the drama that she had been through. She was more upset that they did not call her to let her know that they had stopped payment on the loan and that the house was in jeopardy. Anita could have made the payments herself, but she did not know that they were not being paid. The whole time the police officers was visiting the house they had been bring notices of foreclosure, and they knew Bruce was the only adult home that's why they asked for him. He had warrants so he never talked to them, so no one really knew that the house was in jeopardy until it was to late.

About a year after Anita lost the house on Sugar Hill she left her husband Mr. Willis and ended up coming home to live with her mother. Henry had passed and Rosey was growing in age, so Anita moved on the top floor of the duplex above Rosey making it more convenient for her to care for her mother. The drugs and the hustlers were out of her life. With things much calmer she went back to work as a physical therapist for a rich white family on the south side of town. April and the children were content with her new husband Mr. Charles, and Bruce was headed for self-destruction.

April's new husband, Mr. Charles, was the first man in her life who wanted her to be someone besides 'Ms. Pretty'. He first sent her to Beauty College where she received her beautician's license. Then she went into business for herself and made good money designing and dressing up wigs. Mr. Charles felt April still had too much time on her hands and sent her to Michigan State University to study Early Child-hood Education while he, Anita, Rosey, and other family members took care of the children. April became an independent mother working as a teacher and doing wigs on the side. She tired of living the rich high-class lifestyle and left Mr. Charles with whom she had two more children, although both died. She and the children had finally made it to the top. April left the teaching field and went to work as a rehab specialist at the local Correctional Rehabilitation Center. She became the first black woman to build a house in the business district of Dayton's biggest high-class Jewish neighborhood.

When April had finally gained some respect for herself she fell in love with a General Motors workingman who was a lunatic. At work,

April carried a badge and a gun all day only to come home to be battered by her husband Rick. He was the kind of man who could put the whole house in an uproar. April, Rick, and the children would be eating dinner, and his plate would fly up against the wall because the food did not have enough salt. When they all sat down to play family games and he didn't win, he would flip over the table. He had April so afraid, she would sit in her bedroom without moving for five or six hours after he left for work. He caused her to lose a little dignity, but her longer hours at work helped her deal with this abusive relationship.

Sparkle, Young Gold's mother, had left home two years into her mother's marriage to Rick, but she would call home to check on things often. One day she called, and her brother Eric answered the phone. All of the other children were gone. "Hey, what's going on?" she asked. Eric answered, "I'm ready to kill this fool over here." "Is he still beating on mama?" Sparkle asked. Thirty minutes later Sparkle was at her mother's front door with a loaded 38-caliber pistol tucked into her pants. Rick stopped beating April and made her answer the door. Sparkle came in raving, "I'm tired of you putting your hands on my mama!" Rick rushed to the door and grabbed both Sparkle and April. He had a manhandling grip on both of them. Sparkle was reaching into her pants for her gun, but when Rick turned them around, away from the door, Eric shot him in the face with a 22-caliber pistol. Sparkle, Eric, and April ran out of the house, across the street to a neighbor's house to phone the police. There were over sixty calls on record from April and her neighbors recording her beatings, so no charges were filed.

After April's marriage to Rick, she gave up on seriously becoming involved with men because now, in Young Gold, she had one of her own. She gave all her love to him because she knew there was something special about him. She wanted her grandson to know she was somebody important in the world when he got older. So she started traveling with some of the top R&B artists of the '80's and soon became a lyricist. By the time Young Gold came into the world, his great-grandma Anita was with a man name Emerson Pole, but they did not ever marry throughout their 22-year-long relationship because he already had a wife. Throughout Young Gold's life, Emerson came closest to being a great-grandfather because he was the only man Gold knew to be in his great-grandma Anita's life. It was hard to tell that Emerson had a wife because he spent most of his time doing for Anita and her family. He was very special to the whole family. Gold recalled the times when Emerson would take him, his cousins Vee and Joe Joe, far out to an old white couple's farm to buy spring water for his great-grandma Anita and his great-great-grandma Rosey. They would load the car with thirty empty gallon milk jugs and bring them back filled with fresh spring water.

Emerson always stressed health and hygiene. He did all of Anita's grocery shopping, gardening, cleaning, and laundry. But he played a bigger role in Gold's younger cousin K.C's life because Emerson became like a father to him from the day Anita brought him home from the hospital. Young Gold was about fourteen when Emerson died. He knew his great-grandma Anita and the family would miss the things Emerson did for them, but Gold felt most sorry for K.C because Emerson was really all he had.

Chapter 19

By recalling what he already knew, and by interviewing both his great-grandma Anita and his grandma April, Young Gold gathered reliable information about his family roots that could answer so many questions he had been asking since he was six years old. But to know why his parents had split up would complete his quest. He had never heard them bad talk each other, so he had to poke around to find out what happened.

Around the time Sparkle got pregnant with Young Gold, Brad started to hang out with her Uncle Bruce. She hated when her Uncle came around because she did not want his lifestyle to rub off on Brad. She loved Brad with all of her heart because he was not a man from the streets. She had grown up around pimps and hustlers, and she had fallen for Brad because he was different. But by the time Young Gold was born, Brad had been highly influenced by Bruce. Bruce would come by their house and give Brad packages of heroin, money, and anything else he wanted. Brad did not know anything about the street. He saw how Bruce had lots of women, nice cars, and money, so he gave the streets a chance and started hustling. Brad got in the streets and made a fair amount of money, but he forgot about home. He would stay out all night partying with his friends and drinking while Sparkle and Young Gold were home alone. Sparkle dealt with the situation for the first two years of Gold's life because she knew how it felt to grow up without a father in the early years of life. She tried to do everything in her power to work things out with Brad. Then one day she came downstairs while he had over a house full of friends and saw him put a needle in his arm. She had just recently lost her Uncle Bruce to a death involving a dose of bad dope at the early age of thirty-five, so when she saw Bruce shooting dope she lost her mind. She went on a rampage, yelling, throwing things at him, spitting on him while he just sat there in another world, because he was so high. Sparkle packed her and Young Gold's things and never looked back.

When Young Gold finished his research and study of his family roots, he felt like he had looked in a mirror that reflected his whole life because everything was the same. He also wondered how things would have turned out if his mother had stuck it out with his father and tried to help him, instead of bringing three lunatics into his life from outside of the family. Gold now knew why things had gone the way they had so far, but he was still unsure how to steer things in the right direction for his generation, the next generation, and the ones that had come before. But at least he did have one of his goals in hand that he wanted to accomplish by the age of twenty-five.

Young Gold was doing outstanding work in his second year at U.C. At the end of the spring quarter he came home for the summer with all A's. He knew the OLE Man was proud of him, but he needed help to accomplish his goal of putting the family back together. He had been distant from the family because of school, so he started having family picnics and dinners every week just to bring them all together. After about three weeks, the family faded away again. It was just Gold, his grandma April, and the children of his generation left attending. Gold soon realized that he was only human, and the task that he was trying to complete was going to take someone with much more power than he had, so he called on God. Every night he asked God, "Please bring the positive people in my family into the circle that you and I share, so they can enjoy the love and happiness that it's filled with." Young Gold had faith that everything would come together in all due time, so he continued to work on the family house and enjoy his summer. A majority of the children in his generation came to the house and stayed the weekends that summer, but during the week Gold began to get bored. The OLE Man had been on his mind a lot. Then one day, his grandma April called him in an uproar to tell him about the dream she had the night before about the OLE Man. He had gracefully appeared to her singing a beautiful song. Then he spoke, "You need to quit worrying about your children; they are grown. You need to put your energy into your grandchildren." Young Gold thought his grandma was going crazy at first, but then she sang the song the OLE Man had sung to her in her dream. He almost dropped the phone; the song was so beautiful. More than anything in the world Gold wanted his grandma back into her song writing. For one, he wanted to meet some of the famous musicians and artists that she used to work with, and secondly, he wanted her to get her life back. He also thought about the money she could make. He figured if she wrote a few hit songs, he would not have to worry about how he was going to pay for his last two years of school. But he first had to get her mind off her children.

Every day when Gold talked to his Grandma April, he would ask her about her career as a lyricist. He could hear the glow in her voice in every story she told him. She could see how interested Young Gold was about music, so she brought him many different books about the music business and how to write hit songs. Then one day Gold thought about the research he had done on his ancestry. He realized that his family's bloodline ran through the entertainment world. Many of Gold's family members succeeded in the music industry, and many more had potential to be there if drugs weren't in the way. Young Gold had finally figured out how to put his family back on the road that the drugs had pulled them from. But there were still two things that he had to deal with before his plans would work smoothly.

To put his plans in motion, Young Gold had to first convince his grandma April that sitting out of school that coming fall quarter would not make him lose his focus on his education. "It don't matter how successful my plans turn out to be; I know that I need my education to fall back on," Gold explained. It put a lot of stress on her to accept Gold's decision. But once she thought it through, she realized Gold had been in the same situation before, and that this time he was sitting out for something positive, not for the streets.

The second thing Gold had to deal with was Silver. Gold felt that Silver had to be removed from Sparkle's life because Gold wanted her to be a part of his success. She did not have the power to put Silver out of her life by herself because of the drug addiction, so Gold took matters into his own hands. Before Young Gold even discussed his plans with his mother he told her how he felt about the way Silver had been treating her. Gold knew he had to clean her up and get her mind on the right level before she could complete the required work he had in mind for her. So he gave her two weeks to remove Silver from her life, and told her if she didn't, he was going to kill him. Gold could not deal with the way Sparkle was being treated now that he knew all about his family's history. The two weeks' deadline that he gave her went by like two days because Gold was excited about the things he had planned for the family. Gold thought he needed his mother to be a part of it, and he knew it would never work with Silver in the way.

That Saturday when Sparkle's time was up, Young Gold called her about 8 o'clock. "Did you do it yet?" "I told him he had to leave last night," she answered. Then the next day Young Gold called again, and Silver answered the telephone. He passed it to Sparkle and Young Gold asked calmly, "What happened?" then hung up the phone. She quickly called her mother in a panic. "Mama, what is wrong with my son?" Sparkle asked. "We have big plans, and he is just tired of the shit that's been going on with the family, so you better do whatever it is he is telling you." April advised. Young Gold drove around for about two hours that night full of fire. He made three or four trips back and forth home picking his gun up and dropping it back off, debating if he should go kill Silver or not. Then, after his last trip out of the house without his gun, he went to his grandma April's house in tears. She had known what he was going through, so she asked Gold, "It's not even worth risking all the good things God has filled your life with, is it?" He just broke out in more tears hugging her tight. All he kept thinking about was his Uncle Eric and his mother trying to kill April's husband Rick when they wanted him out of their lives. Young Gold was trying to change things for his generation, so the next day he stepped to Silver toe-to-toe and said, "I don't appreciate the way you have disrespected my mother and my family." Silver tried to speak, but Gold cut him off, then added, "I'm a grown man now, and I'm not going to sit back and watch you kill my mother and destroy my family with that shit. The best thing for you to do is to stay away from her, and I will bring you all your materials and possessions," Gold stated. Ever since Silver had come home from prison he had seen the power Young Gold possessed, so he obeyed his wishes.

For the rest of the summer up until the middle of the fall season, Young Gold studied and read all the books his grandma April brought him about the entertainment world. He found out there was a lot of hard work involved in creating a hit song because the process of putting a song together involved many people. His Grandma April always said, "Pay yourself first." So Gold did his best to learn about every job involved in the business. He saw that the less number of people involved in making a song or album was better for financial and safety reasons. He witnessed his grandma lose her first hit song, and he read about a few entertainers losing out on their first hit songs. There was one person he read about who had been beaten out of $78,000 because the record company he was working with went out of business. But from that point on, that particular entertainer learned how to complete every job in the business himself, so he would not lose out a second time. Young Gold felt he had already lost his first piece of money in the music industry when his grandma lost her song. Gold was already two steps ahead of the game because he learned from his grandma's mistake, and from all the entertainers he read about. He tackled the books about the music business just as he did his schoolbooks. With the knowledge that he gained from his studying, and the musical genes that flowed though his body, he knew he was going to be successful in the business. His first collection included over thirty-five songs. Then he pulled all the children of his generation that were involved with the family together and started rehearsing songs with them. He even had his son Roland J. on a few songs that he had put together.

When Young Gold's grandma April came to the family house one Sunday to hear Young Gold and her other grandchildren practice, she almost came out of remission. She was so excited that night she went home leaving messages for old friends in the music industry, big-time entertainment lawyers, and production companies to call her. Young Gold had put his grandma back on her high horse again. After she contacted people spreading her joy, she thought about how she lost her own song, and decided this time around she would do everything herself. She wanted to run her own record company, so she and Young Gold planned to build a recording studio in some of the extra space at the family house. But in order to fund the project Gold needed his mother's help.

Two or more months had passed before Young Gold and his grandma dropped the bomb on Sparkle. They had gone out with some of April's earnings from bingo and bought over a thousand dollars worth of silk and polyester fabric, and other sewing materials. Young Gold had designed a line of men's loungewear that included boxer shorts, house pants, long sleeve shirts, 3/4-length and full-length robes. Sparkle was not enthusiastic about the idea at first, but she would do anything for Gold's education. He and his grandma would never mentioned the studio to her because they knew she would not work as hard if she knew what they were really trying to raise money for. Besides, they saw sewing as a way to keep her mind off of the drugs. The sewing started off fair, but when the idea crashed Gold refused to give up. He was too close to completing his goals to give up, so he called on the Lord again.

Gold had really started to believe and recognize the power of God through prayer. All that he prayed for came to pass. It was like when the OLE Man died, a new power was born inside of Gold. April had put her life back on a professional level. And even though his mother had not fully come around from the drugs he could see a consistent change in her lifestyle. The things Gold started to see in his mother and grandma added more fuel and encouragement in his life. He was just about to reach the age in his life when everything had fallen apart for them. But he already had his mind set on what he wanted in life, and continued exploring his entrepreneurial ideas in clothing designs, writing songs, and working on his degree in education.

Gold was not able to fix the past. But by learning about it and living through it, he would be able to guide his generation and the ones to follow. There was no way he would allow the family to get as far off track as it was. And he never wanted to encounter the things he had been through before, or the things that his grandparent, parents, aunts, and uncles had been through. But the most important thing to Young Gold was making a better life for all of the children under him because they were promised to be stars. He did not want to see his generation follow the same steps, repeating the circle of destruction as had the previous generations.

The women who raised Young Gold were proud of him even though they had known he was something special from the start. On his twenty-fifth birthday he received the greatest gift ever. He was surrounded by all the special women in his life, his great-grandmother Anita, his grandmother April, his mother Sparkle, his aunts Mica and China, his sister, and his own baby girl Diamond. As they all sang happy birthday to Gold and the candles were blown out, all the women said in voices filled with relief, "Somebody had to come up with something."

The End

Coming Soon The Album:

"His Name Is Gold"

www.ingramcontent.com/pod-product-compliance
Lightning Source LLC
Chambersburg PA
CBHW052035270326
41931CB00012B/2497